MW01469846

Mark
Andrews

Ian
Jordaan

Cyril
Beeka

Lolly
Jackson

George
Smith

LOLLY JACKSON
WHEN FANTASY BECOMES REALITY

Sean Newman, Peter Piegl
and Karyn Maughan

JACANA

First published by Jacana Media (Pty) Ltd in 2012

10 Orange Street
Sunnyside
Auckland Park 2092
South Africa
+2711 628 3200
www.jacana.co.za

ISBN 978-1-4314-0296-0

Also available as an e-book
d-PDF ISBN 978-1-4314-0343-1
ePUB ISBN 978-1-4314-0353-0
mobi file ISBN 978-1-4314-0354-7

Cover design by publicide
Set in Sabon 11/16pt
Printed by Ultra Litho (Pty) Ltd, Johannesburg
Job no. 001679

See a complete list of Jacana titles at www.jacana.co.za

Every effort has been made to ensure the accuracy of details, names, facts, places and events contained in this book. In the event of any inaccuracy, the authors and publisher welcome feedback. Some names may have been changed or removed for privacy.

For Alexis, my angel and guiding light in all the darkness
— S.N.

CONTENTS

A brief note before reading this book

Sometimes the most fascinating books are those that have a range of voices that contribute to the telling of the story. Having three authors is both a challenge and a delight – and most certainly never dull.

Part I recounts Sean Newman's personal journey into the world of Lolly Jackson, his experiences of working with Lolly at Teazers, and the aftermath of Lolly's murder – using information to which few people had access.

Part II is *eNews* investigative journalist Karyn Maughan's uncovering of the diabolical tax mess, complicated financial dealings and the web of characters, living and dead, that surrounded Lolly Jackson.

Part III Sean Newman describes the shocking killings that followed Lolly's murder, including Ian Jordaan and Mark Andrews.

ABOUT THE AUTHORS

Sean Newman began working for Lolly a year before his death. He lived the Teazers' brand and became integral in not only the day-to-day operations as media, marketing and public relations manager, but also as a keen observer of everything that really happened. While others wrote about the Teazers' lifestyle, Newman lived it.

Peter Piegl was the editor of *Playboy South Africa* until mid-2011 and is the writing power behind the book. Piegl brings a critical and textured approach to the story.

Karyn Maughan is an award-winning legal reporter who began her career working at a mortuary. After four years of reporting for *The Star*, she began working at *eNews*, where she has gained a reputation as one of the country's top crime journalists. She's been named one of South Africa's most influential journalists on Twitter.

CAST OF CHARACTERS

Agliotti, Glenn — Convicted drug dealer and friend of Radovan Krejcir

Allschwang, Alan — Lolly Jackson's tax attorney

Andrews, Mark — Ex-Teazers' partner involved in a legal dispute over ownership of Teazers Cresta

Beeka, Cyril — Security boss and associate of Radovan Krejcir

De Jager, Paul — Lolly Jackson's business partner (in the Midrand Property holding company)

Fabre, Nichol — Ricardo Fabre's fiancée, later wife

Fabre, Ricardo — Teazers' financial manager and Lolly's right hand

Fedele, Greg — Lolly Jackson's partner at Teazers Cape Town

Fensham, Sharon Tracy — Lolly Jackson's second wife

Gavrić, Dubrosav (*aka Sasa Kovacić*) — Alleged assassin of Željko 'Arkan' Ražnotović; Beeka's driver during assassination

Gemballa, Uwe — German supercar converter

Jackson, Demi — Lolly Jackson's third wife (born Belinda Megan Snyman)

Jackson, Julian — Lolly Jackson's son with his second wife, Sharon Fensham

Jackson, Lolly — King of Teaze (born Emmanuel Zachary)

Jackson, Manoli — Lolly Jackson's son with his first wife, Vivian Starkey

Jackson, Samantha	Lolly Jackson's daughter with his first wife, Vivian Starkey
Jordaan, Ian	Lolly Jackson's attorney
Kalymnios, Michael	Teazers' client who was romantically involved with a former Teazers' dancer
Krejcir, Radovan	Czech fugitive, named by the media as suspect in Cyril Beeka's murder
Mabasa, Major General Khanyisa 'Joey'	Crime Intelligence boss (former, given a gold handshake on his way out)
Manson, Tyrel	Demi Jackson's high-school sweetheart, with whom she allegedly became romantically involved while married to Lolly Jackson
Newman, Samantha	Sean Newman's wife
O'Sullivan, Paul	Forensic investigator and security consultant looking into the murders of people associated with Lolly Jackson
Panayi, Alekos	Former bank manager, Laiki Bank
Phillips, Andrew	Owner of rival strip club, The Grand
Russouw, Shaun	Lolly Jackson's partner at Teazers Durban
Smith, George (aka George Louka)	Prime suspect in Lolly Jackson's murder
Teixeira, Robyn	Lolly Jackson's personal assistant

PART I

1
LOLLY'S MURDER

Monday, 3 May 2010

'Fuck off!' Lolly Jackson's last words to me echoed in my mind. It was a cold evening in May 2010, and I was standing apprehensively on an unfamiliar driveway in Kempton Park. Fine rain gently settled on my skin, and all I could think of were those two curt words. They were spoken in the flush of anger and would be the last exchange to pass between us. Lolly was more than just my employer; he was a man I'd grown to love and respect, and who I'd asked to be my child's godfather. All that remained now was a shattered corpse that belied the controversial, larger-than-life personality that had birthed an empire. Agonisingly, the truth was taking hold; our King of Teaze was dead.

The night Lolly Jackson died began like any other. I was tucked up warmly in bed and my wife had just finished putting our three-month-old daughter to sleep after her feed. My cellphone rang unexpectedly. Jarred awake, I rolled over, grumbling, and vaguely registered the name on the screen – Imraan Karolia from *Eyewitness News*. A call from the press during the night was commonplace and I rolled my eyes, thinking that Lolly had been arrested again. The conversation that followed made me wish that had been the case.

Sean:	Yes, Imraan?
Imraan:	Hi Sean, sorry to disturb you.
Sean:	No problem, what's up?
Imraan:	Sean, can you confirm or deny that Lolly Jackson is dead?

His statement sucked the air out of my lungs. Disbelief intermingled with fear and helplessness as I launched out of bed and ran out of the room – searching for a clearer cellphone signal. Maybe I'd heard wrong...

Sean:	What? What the hell are you talking about? Imraan, what's going on?
Imraan:	Sean, we've had word from multiple sources that Lolly has been killed tonight. Can you confirm or deny this for us?
Sean:	Are you sure it's not a prank?
Imraan:	It has come from a few sources and they are all very credible.
Sean:	Are you sure? Where?
Imraan:	We can't confirm; that's why we're calling you. Apparently he was shot somewhere in Kempton Park, a house.

Sean:	Imraan, hold the story! I don't care how you do it, just hold it. Let me make some calls and then phone me back ASAP. Get me an address, please!
Imraan:	I will hold, but we need confirmation from you.
Sean:	Get me an address and I'll go right now. I'll confirm.

Shaking, I put the phone down and stumbled outside to have a cigarette. I desperately called both of Lolly's numbers, but they just rang and went to voicemail. Each call brought with it a sense of impending doom; Lolly was *never* unavailable.

I walked slowly back inside and told my concerned wife that Lolly might be dead. As the words tumbled from my mouth, I grabbed my phone from my pocket and began to search for Ricardo Fabre's number. He was Teazers' financial manager and was hard-wired into the goings-on in the business. No doubt he'd dismiss the story as utter nonsense, saying he'd just heard from Lolly and that they'd laughed about getting yet more free mileage over this latest controversy.

Ricardo answered, his voice betraying his own doubts and concerns. He explained he'd heard from our Cape Town partner, Greg Fedele, that something was seriously wrong; that possibly Lolly had been shot but was still alive. I was becoming increasingly anxious. I agreed to touch base shortly after calling Lolly's attorney, Ian Jordaan who, if anyone, would know the truth. But Ian had no further insight to offer.

I reasoned with myself that there was no possible way Lolly Jackson could be dead. He was too well known and connected to some of the most powerful and feared men in the country. While mulling this over and trying to remain controlled, the phone rang. Not recognising the number, I prepared myself for the onslaught of yet more journalists, but the hysterical voice on the other end of the line caught me off guard: it was Demi – Lolly's estranged wife.

Sobbing, she asked where her husband was. I told her nothing had been confirmed yet, but she'd be the first person I'd call when I had some facts in hand. At least I now had her cellphone number – this had changed when she and Lolly had separated acrimoniously and he'd cancelled her cellphone contract.

I'd barely put the phone down when an SMS came through from Imraan – it was the one I'd so anxiously been waiting for. It stated simply: 'Sean, 25 Joan Hunter Avenue, Edleen'. It also had the Sebenza Police Station's number and ended off with the word 'hurry'.

Quickly getting dressed and preparing to leave for Kempton Park, I called Ricardo and Lolly's personal assistant, Robyn Teixeira. Ricardo was en route to Teazers Rivonia to fetch Manoli, Lolly's son from his marriage to his first wife, Vivian Starkey. Robyn and her husband Manny were packing their son into the car and had made plans to fetch Demi. They were originally going to meet at a pre-arranged spot so that they could go to the crime scene together, but Demi's car had hit a pothole, forcing her to wait to be collected at a petrol station nearby.

Rushing to the address in a speeding taxi, I replayed the day's events in my head. I'd woken with a painful ache in my neck. I'd met Ricardo for coffee before work and had told him I needed to see a doctor. Ricardo had said he was going to take time off to sign papers for a loan to buy a restaurant. After roughly a decade of working at Teazers, he'd finally be the captain of his own ship.

My doctor had booked me off for two days so I called Lolly to let him know, but his terse answer betrayed he was in a worse mood than usual. My sickness, along with Ricardo's 'absenteeism', was coming under scrutiny from our capricious boss. Adding to Lolly's frustration was the dismal cellphone signal. He shouted, 'Fuck off!' at the cellphone service provider and ended the call. When he phoned back I tried to explain my situation, but received the same disturbing expletive in return.

Lolly's cycle of bad moods had begun to intensify. I've often wondered whether this was the result of an inner voice alerting him to the fact that his life was in danger or merely due to the stress of his imminent divorce from Demi. After his death, Robyn and I would sit together and reminisce. She said Lolly was acting strangely on the day of his murder: 'He picked up the phone and called my husband [Manny]. He asked me how my son was doing and that was just totally out of character.'

I found out later that Shaun Russouw – Lolly's partner at Teazers Durban – had received a similar call that day. After asking about Shaun's wife and child, Lolly spat, 'I've told the bitch to fuck off' – an apparent reference to Demi. Lolly's mood had also become clear to handyman Lacksom Makhalina who had seen a 'very worried, very stressed' Lolly repeatedly riding his scooter up and down the driveway of his Kyalami home that last morning.

As the taxi hurtled towards the address Imraan had sent me, I tried to work out why it seemed familiar. On arriving, I stood in the shadows some distance away from the scene, considering whether I should turn around and leave. My trepidation was building – as much as I needed to know the truth, I was terrified of what I might learn. As I took those first tentative steps onto the open driveway, I saw a large man talking to two people near a car. A woman turned, microphone in hand, and I sensed that some terrible truth was about to be revealed. She introduced herself as Mandy Wiener and greeted me by name. I saw her lips move but I couldn't hear a thing. As I turned to face the authoritative man, who introduced himself as Colonel Eugene Opperman, her words filtered through my mind: 'I'm sorry.'

'Don't tell me it's my boss,' I begged, but he confirmed my worst fears. I collapsed on the driveway, crying.

As I got up unsteadily, Mandy approached and asked if I was able to give a comment. I said I would, but needed to gather my composure first. Mandy told me the story was about to break live on air and my body stiffened. I told her we couldn't do that as Lolly's family hadn't yet been informed, but she said it was too late. She offered me her phone (as my battery had finally died) so I could try to contact Demi as I'd promised. I grabbed it and dialled the number, unwittingly giving Mandy direct access to Lolly's estranged wife.

Demi answered and all I can remember telling her, through body-wracking tears, was that Lolly was dead. I just kept saying 'sorry' and 'he's dead'. Only the next morning did I realise – when I heard the grief-stricken conversation replayed on *Talk Radio 702* – that Mandy, the intrepid reporter, had surreptitiously recorded my end of the conversation with Demi.

I desperately needed a cigarette. I wanted the safety of solitude, but I had a job to do. Lolly had trusted me for a reason, and I felt duty-bound to fulfil my responsibilities, no matter what.

◉

I was summoned by Colonel Opperman, who said there was a police officer wanting to speak to me in private. I climbed into a silver sedan and noticed a plain-clothes officer sitting with a docket in the driver's seat. It would later transpire that the man was in fact none other than Gauteng Crime Intelligence boss Major General Khanyisa 'Joey' Mabasa.

He began by asking if I knew the deceased, to which I nodded. He then enquired who the victim was. This totally threw me as the police themselves had only moments prior confirmed who it was to *me*! I told him it was Lolly Jackson. The police officer looked down and noted something in the docket.

His next question completely astonished me: he asked who Lolly Jackson was! All I could do was point to the Teazers' badge on my shirt pocket, mouth agape in disbelief. The police officer nodded and started to brief me about what I was allowed to say to the press.

I was utterly stunned. A few seconds earlier, the officer had pretended not to know who Lolly was or that he was dead, yet he was well aware that it was my job to talk to the press! Either the man had just experienced an epiphany or I was a pawn in some sort of sick game (I later discovered Lolly had Joey Mabasa's contact details saved on his cellphone). I listened in a daze as he instructed me not to bad-mouth the police in any way. Under no circumstances was I to talk about the crime or change my commentary to anything other than: 'We have full faith in the police and the manner in which they are conducting this investigation.'

Angry and confused, I got out of the car just as Ricardo arrived on the scene along with Peter Burner (head of the Sandton Police Reservist Division), Father Keith (police chaplain) and Manoli, looking as pale as he did the day he contracted an infection after his appendix was removed.

I embraced the shattered Manoli, then ushered him over to the paramedics who had arrived to assist with trauma counselling.

A screeching wail suddenly cleaved the cold night air. Demi had begun to climb out of Robyn's car before it had even stopped. She stumbled while running and fell to her knees in the middle of the road. Screaming, 'Where is my man? What was he doing here?' She was quickly ushered over to the paramedics to join Manoli. Grief can manifest itself in the strangest ways. Demi's reaction on arriving at the murder scene seemed a sharp contrast to the story Robyn would later tell me. As Robyn described it, when she and Manny had arrived at the garage to collect Demi, Lolly's wife had been chatting amiably with the forecourt attendants. But the moment she'd laid eyes on Robyn and Manny, Demi had collapsed in a sobbing heap.

In emotional turmoil, Ricardo and I walked away, not wanting to intrude in family matters. At that moment two men, who would later be closely linked to the murder investigation, arrived: Czech fugitive Radovan Krejcir and security boss and underworld kingpin Cyril Beeka. Ironically, Cyril would himself die in a hail of bullets almost one year later to the day.

After chatting to Radovan and Cyril, Ricardo and I turned back towards the crime scene and saw the door to the house open. From where we were standing, I had a clear view of the interior of the entrance hall, albeit a brief one. The police had congregated near the doorway that led directly into the garage. There were two short steps up to a medium-sized passageway leading to what appeared to be an open-plan lounge. I was immediately struck by the sight of an arched smear of blood on the wall, approximately 60–80 cm in length. All the signs told me that Lolly had been shot while trying to get away and had stumbled down the steps, reaching out for support, but his legs had failed him. With tears welling in my eyes again, I turned away.

The autopsy report would later reveal the exact details of the devastation inflicted on Lolly Jackson's body. The official cause of death has been cited as 'multiple bullet wounds'. Lolly was shot twice over the left posterior chest wall which resulted in a fractured rib and a perforated lobe of his left lung. Another bullet entered his left lateral chest wall, perforating his diaphragm and entering his stomach. Two shots were fired into the parietal region of his head – bullet and bone fragments causing additional trauma to his already mortally wounded brain. The sixth shot entered 3 cm in front of Lolly's left ear. This was executed at close range, resulting in 'tattooing' of the skin from the gunpowder. Clearly, this had been the killer's last – and was intended to ensure his target was stone dead.

Lolly's shirtless body (the shirt was never found) with his jeans pulled down around his legs would be delivered later to the mortuary. The autopsy would reveal that this was not due to sexual abuse of any sort, so I imagine that his corpse must have been dragged – causing Lolly's jeans to slip down without his belt breaking. It would later come to light that he'd been living on borrowed time, as forensic pathologist Johannes Steenkamp noted that his heart was enlarged and showed signs of severe cardiac disease. The 53-year-old had been on the brink of heart failure.

Shaking, I walked away from Ricardo and the scene before me, wanting to remember Lolly as the strong man he'd always been.

Ricardo and I saw Robyn and her family off as she left to take Demi home, and then walked to the top of the driveway. I reiterated that this address was, for some reason, familiar. He suggested that it might have been some project Lolly and I had worked on together, because he didn't know who stayed there. Prior to receiving the SMS from me, he hadn't even known the place existed.

Ricardo was on the phone to Lolly's lawyer, Ian Jordaan, debriefing him, when it suddenly hit me. This was George Smith's place! – 'FAT George', as Lolly had aptly saved him in his phone.

Addicted to crack, George Smith was a petty criminal who was elevated into a world of ego and power after becoming friends with cellmate Radovan Krejcir in 2007. The two ended up in the same prison cells, despite their frequent change of venues, and Radovan saw this as kismet. George became the go-to guy – a man to whom Radovan and Lolly could turn to get things done. This address had appeared at the top of an affidavit he'd written for Lolly while my boss was in jail as a result of the Michael Kalymnios case. (Lolly had been arrested in February 2010 for allegedly trying to extort money from Michael, who was dating a former Teazers' dancer. George later stated in his affidavit that Michael had offered him money to falsely claim that Lolly was going to hire him to kill Michael.)

As these thoughts went through my mind, Ricardo continued his conversation with Ian. I interrupted and asked him to hand me his phone. After telling Ian what I knew, he argued that it was Michael who lived in Kempton Park while George lived in Kensington, but I stood firm and corrected him and he agreed to check the address in the morning.

By this time, Colonel Opperman was addressing the media gathered on the opposite side of the road from the house, and Ricardo told me to join them and make a statement. To this day I don't know how I managed to utter a word, let alone string a sentence together.

After mumbling something, I returned to the paramedics to find Manoli, who was insisting on viewing his father's body. Like Lolly, he had a stubborn streak and a sceptical nature which meant he wouldn't believe his father was dead until he could verify this for himself. We all desperately tried to persuade him not to do so, but he insisted. Just after midnight, he was escorted inside the house by Father Keith. Ricardo followed Manoli but came out almost immediately. When Manoli emerged, the expression on his face was one of utter horror and devastation. He was clutching a plastic shopping bag containing his father's bloodied watch, chain and crucifix, as if someone might seize it from him at any moment. I noticed that his knuckles were almost opaque. We all climbed into the car that Peter Burner had reversed into the driveway and solemnly left for Teazers Rivonia. Ricardo and I sat in the back flanking Manoli, who wouldn't let the shopping bag out of his grasp. It was at this point that I realised the plastic bag was branded with the Pick n Pay logo. The irony was not lost on me – I kept thinking that if Lolly were here, he would have flown into a rage, knowing his most prized possessions were in a shopping bag carrying the brand of the same company that had forced him to close his Bedfordview branch and spawned numerous altercations with its CEO, Sean Summers.

When we arrived at Teazers, the lights were still on inside. The red eyes of the remaining few customers stared back at us, completely oblivious to the horror of the past few hours. The night's events had taken a heavy toll on us. I quietly excused myself and left for home and its relative safety. I couldn't stay at Teazers any longer. Lolly had been the heart and soul of this business and without his charismatic presence, it suddenly felt to me as if someone had reached in and ripped the life out of it, reducing it to nothing more than bricks and mortar.

I arrived home to a family waiting to comfort me, but what I needed most was some time alone. I had a shower in the vain hope that the scalding water would wash away all I'd seen and experienced that night. Having sought the solitude of a quiet room, I cried for the man who had saved my family from financial ruin, who had given me hope and who had restored my dignity.

The fantasy was over.

2

THE KING OF TEAZE:
WOMEN, WHEELS AND POKER

To the outside world, Lolly Jackson was the embodiment of the devil – a shady businessman who had questionable friends and who had been arrested on several occasions for alleged crimes ranging in severity from assault to human trafficking. To add fuel to this fire, Lolly offered no excuses for his life of excess. He glutted himself on fast cars and even faster women, and cared little for consequence or popular opinion. His megalomania sometimes offended the public and Lolly himself encouraged certain misconceptions as there were parts of himself that he was at pains to hide. Robyn Teixeira, who had worked closely with Lolly for many years, says he was simply misunderstood: 'Lolly chose to be that way. He was a vulnerable man and he took everything to heart.'

Over time I learnt that Lolly Jackson was a complex being and it was this complexity that contributed to the downward spiral of his turbulent life. Lolly was driven, confrontational, and demanded loyalty and obedience. He was ultimately ruled by a cruel taskmaster – his ego – and it needed to be fed. Lolly *had* to be known – feared, respected or loathed; he cared little either way. To Lolly, anonymity was unacceptable.

The man known to South Africans as Lolly Jackson began his life on 24 September 1956 as Emmanuel Zachary. He was born in Elizabethville in the Belgian Congo to Greek parents, George and Soula. Soula ran a small general dealer store and George was the owner of a Texaco petrol station.

In 1960, after weeks of violent riots which left hundreds dead, the country achieved independence and became known as Zaire. Violence continued, mobs ransacked businesses and the Zachary family decided to flee. George reinforced their 1950s Oldsmobile and they broke through the border-post barricades and fled south to safety, eventually settling in Germiston, east of Johannesburg. In an effort to assimilate the family with their new community, George changed their surname to Jackson. It was Soula who renamed Emmanuel. On returning from three months basic training in the SANDF, a highly excited Soula began shouting that 'Lolly' was home (Lolly being a diminutive of Emmanuel) and this expression, much to her son's chagrin, was echoed by a friend. From that moment on, Emmanuel Zachary was no more.

Around the time Lolly was 22, he met and started dating Vivian Starkey. After a year, Vivian fell pregnant. Driven by a code of responsibility inculcated by his parents, Lolly married Vivian in 1980. Their son George was born soon after but tragically, only four months later, the baby succumbed to cot death.

A distraught Lolly was beside himself and, with what later became his trademark explosive temper already in place, he started upending desks and furniture at work. Later, when grief replaced his anger, he was found sitting at the morgue, refusing to move until staff had to throw him out. Caught up in a personal hell, Lolly blamed Vivian for the tragedy. In the years that followed, the pain receded and two more children were born, Samantha and Manoli. Within six years, however, the marriage was in trouble and the couple divorced in 1986.

As I spent more time with Lolly, I witnessed his wariness of the fairer sex. I think it had a lot to do with his traditional Greek upbringing, where men are deemed superior to women. Lolly subscribed to this mindset, and I believe his wariness had more to do with Lolly feeling that women couldn't do a man's job, rather than pure distrust.

In 1990 Lolly met his second wife, Sharon Tracy Fensham, while she was working as a receptionist at Goldstein Attorneys in Germiston. He was a client of the firm and, ever the ladies' man, he started flirting with Sharon the moment he saw her. Sharon's boss, who knew Lolly well, encouraged her to accept his client's invitations to dinner as he saw Lolly as extremely lonely and felt that the company would be good for him. They hit it off after the first date and their meetings became more regular. Lolly was working as a DJ at the time and enjoyed being the life of the party, but he was driven by ambition for greater things and he soon bought a brick and paving factory, making his first million in the years to follow.

Sharon moved in with Lolly five months after that first meeting. The couple were engaged a few times as 'he kept buying me dud rings', Sharon good-naturedly remembers. Lolly would boast that her rings were worth thousands, but she'd later find out that the 'diamonds' were in fact cubic zirconia.

Sharon recalls that they 'had a really good relationship, but it was volatile. He was always playing around and flirting. His whole thing to me was he never had affairs and I had to catch him. I spent my life trying to catch him.'

Once married, Lolly and Sharon moved to 40 Kloof Road in Bedfordview. Lolly's ego dictated that he *had* to live on this street in the affluent suburb, even though their home was quite dilapidated. It took a year to revamp, but Lolly's determination paid off. 'Lolly was passionate about everything he did,' says Sharon. Unfortunately, the price of this passion was Lolly's tempestuous mood swings. The slightest frustration would send him into a rage and he'd destroy anything he could lay his hands on, from cellphones and laptops to furniture.

'Lolly was terrible at fixing things,' Sharon recalls, bemused. 'We didn't even have a proper wall around the property and Lolly was trying to fit the TV into the wall unit. It didn't have a hole in the back to put the wires through; he was trying to force the wires down the side instead. As I turned around, I saw our neighbours walking towards our house in order to introduce themselves. The next minute, the TV goes flying past me! Lolly kicked that unit to pieces.'

Despite the fact that their relationship appeared solid to the outside observer, the marriage came under severe strain because of Lolly's flirtatious nature. He would openly tease women in front of Sharon, writing down girls' telephone numbers on his wife's cigarette boxes. Lolly explained this by saying that he was only trying to keep her interested. Sharon says, 'It actually destroyed me in the end. I had to see a therapist after a while.' It was also difficult for Lolly and Sharon to spend quality time together because of his rigorous work routine, which added to the demise of their relationship.

From the start of their marriage, Sharon had wanted to have a child with Lolly. He wasn't keen as he was already father to Samantha and Manoli. His attitude changed when he suffered a major heart attack. As Sharon walked into the ward shortly after he had been admitted to hospital, she could see that her husband was terrified. He said he wanted to leave her 'with something of me', should anything go wrong in the future.

After falling pregnant with their son Julian, Sharon's trust issues intensified. Just prior to their decision to have a baby, Lolly had opened up a business called the Gold Card Club which was, in effect, a brothel. Despite promising Sharon that he'd only have to go there to collect money, Lolly spent increasing amounts of time there. Sharon never felt comfortable with Lolly's involvement in this business and soon the couple's disagreements escalated to a point that became untenable for Sharon.

Another factor adding further pressure to their relationship was that Lolly was proving to be a poor father. With his old-school Greek notions of parenting, he had no interest in dealing with screaming kids – he liked the *idea* of being a father, but that was it. In his mind, children needed to be seen and not heard, and certainly not to be the cause of stress in his life. His role therefore became solely that of a provider – one he played perhaps too well. In a discussion about inheritance, Sharon mentions that as part of the divorce settlement Lolly had given Vivian a house. When questioning his generosity, friends had been told that it wasn't for Vivian; it was for Samantha and Manoli. 'If he hadn't given everything to the kids, it would have gone to the SPCA,' Sharon says. 'Lolly didn't trust women.' Before his heart surgery, Lolly sat up in bed and rewrote his will while his wife looked on. He left the vast majority of his fortune to his children. He was at pains to make sure his children would be well taken care of. Sharon and Lolly were divorced in 1997.

◉

The first time I met Demi (born Belinda Megan Snyman) was in June 2009, when she arrived at the Teazers Rivonia offices with her mother. Her appearance was super-polished and presentable, and she was swathed in designer-label clothing. On that particular day, she was concerned about a digital camera she had left inside Lolly's Aston Martin DB9, which had since gone in for a service. The problem was that the device had video footage on it of Lolly speeding around the track in one of his supercars, footage that Lolly would certainly want to show to his friends. The camera also contained images of shoddy workmanship that Lolly needed for yet another lawsuit against a building contractor. The possible loss of this material had Demi almost quivering with anxiety and she implored Ricardo to help her locate the camera.

Unfortunately when found, it was a mangled wreck; jammed between the seats of the car, it was now buckled and bent beyond repair. The memory card, too, was damaged. Luckily for Demi, Lolly never asked about it, but she seemed to live in constant fear that he'd remember and take his anger out on her. This relationship wasn't easy. Lolly was tempestuous, controlling and potentially abusive, and the effect would take a toll on his wife.

Stories differ on just how and when Demi met Lolly. In a magazine interview in 2011, Demi said it was in 1996, during a bachelor's party where she was working as a stripper. Lolly saw her and immediately offered her a job at his first Teazers' branch in Primrose – she started work the very next day; the day his branch opened. Two years later, their professional relationship transformed into an intimate one. Demi gave up dancing and became Mrs Jackson in 1999.

However, in the Graeme Moon documentary, filmed in 2008, Demi's story on how she met Lolly is somewhat different. She describes how she was working as a Sun City dancer and only started work at Teazers on their opening night. She went on to say it took four years before she and Lolly became intimate. One indisputable truth remains – Demi was born in January of 1979 and Teazers began trading in 1996, dates which put Demi at a tender 17 years old when she began working as a stripper in the club; if true, a risky endeavour for a venue that would be prone to constant raids.

Demi played the role of wife to perfection, for a while. In September 2009, Lolly decided to combine his (unknown to us then, last) birthday and house-warming party as the couple had only days before moved from Bedfordview to Beaulieu Country Estate in Kyalami. By couple, I actually mean Demi, as she'd single-handedly taken care of the entire move. This had placed a lot of stress on her as she was extremely house-proud (Demi cleaned her house herself). Her desire for cleanliness bordered on the obsessive – she would even vacuum the plug points!

On the day of the party Demi looked spectacular, despite her earlier domestic labouring, but I was soon to see more of the dynamics that made her marriage to Lolly so anxiety-provoking. She was chatting with her guests in the kitchen when Lolly phoned her from the garage. Unhesitatingly, Demi ran out at break-neck speed to see what he wanted. Later, Nichol Fabre said that 'they used to have nights where

21

he [Lolly] went out to play poker and she was allowed a girls' night. If she wasn't home when he got back, there'd be hell to pay, so she'd make sure everyone would phone her when he was leaving the poker game. She'd then race home, jump in the bath and it would look like she'd been home forever, else there'd be big shit.' (*scan QR code 1 on page 218 to listen to this interview*) In terms of their roles within the marriage, Lolly projected the image of the demanding, cold husband and Demi the subservient and perfectionist wife.

And then there were times of blissful love and companionship.

I remember a day in January 2010, when Lolly asked me to come through to his house as Demi needed help connecting a new laptop to the internet. My wife Sam and I found them in the garage. Sitting at a felt-topped table, Lolly was preparing for an online poker tournament. He started telling me about a fight at the club the previous night in which he'd had to intervene. While Lolly was relating this tale, Demi was curled up on the couch to Lolly's right with a huge snack platter she'd prepared for the two of them. They seemed relaxed, in love and enjoying their time together.

Little did we know then that, a few weeks later, the two would be contemplating divorce. This pattern of volatility, of intense make up and break up, would continue throughout their relationship and ultimately be a major factor in the breakdown of their marriage.

If Lolly had been hurt by two failed marriages, a third on the brink of collapse and perceived betrayals by friends and business partners (even when a dancer he hardly knew left Teazers to work elsewhere, he would regard this as a monumental betrayal), he seemed nonetheless determined to hide his vulnerability for fear that it would be perceived as weakness. That rock-hard exterior meant that people were hesitant to mess with him, his family, his girls or his businesses. Terrified that his vulnerabilities would be exposed and used against him, Lolly suffered in silence.

But despite Lolly's mistrust of people, especially women, there was one steadfast, strong-willed woman who entered his life, stood by him for nine years and earned his respect: Robyn Teixeira. Major debt forced Robyn to move from Cape Town to Johannesburg. She needed money urgently and decided to work as a dancer at Teazers. Once her debt had been paid off, she stayed on at Teazers and even resumed stripping after the birth of her child. Later, when Robyn developed a tumour on her chest plate which needed medical attention several times a week, Lolly offered her the opportunity to become his personal assistant. This new position would give her the freedom and financial stability she needed.

Because she worked so closely with him, Robyn could track the change in Lolly's personality. In the beginning, she recalls, 'He was a lot more mellow and he would be involved in the club as a DJ or as a worker. I don't know how, but over time he became more strict and people didn't want to be around him.'

The other 'rock' Lolly relied on heavily was Teazers' financial manager, Ricardo Fabre, a stalwart in Lolly's operation. Ricardo and Lolly worked in completely different ways – Ricardo was organised and meticulous while Lolly was spontaneous, mercurial and easily bored. Ricardo, much like his boss, has a soft side that was only ever exposed on very rare occasions to people he felt comfortable with. As a co-worker, his rules of engagement were strict and he never socialised with the staff unless it was to attend a special event, like Lolly's birthday or my wedding.

Being close to Lolly meant that Ricardo suffered the brunt of Lolly's mood swings; his head bowed in supplication, accepting blame even when the fault didn't lie with him. For a long time, I didn't understand why, but I could only assume that Ricardo had some form of financial arrangement with Lolly (as was the case with me), because no one would otherwise put up with such verbal abuse.

In April 2007, before I began working at the club, Ricardo and Lolly were arrested on charges of fraud and contravening the Immigration Act. As Lolly already had prior convictions, Ricardo was asked to take the fall instead. Afterwards, Ricardo admitted to me that, as payment for his loyalty, he had been given a BMW Z4, among other things, and that Lolly had covered the transfer fees for the house he'd bought.

Ricardo told me of Lolly's love of cars and his collection, housed in the garage of his new Kyalami home, but nothing prepared me for what I saw. The enormous black-tiled floor displayed enough cars and bikes to make an exotic car dealer blush.

His collection of around 22 cars, estimated prior to his death to be worth approximately R96 million, included highly coveted wheels like the Aston Martin DB9, a Dodge Viper, the Corvette Stingray, the Pagani Zonda, the amazing Koenigsegg Competition Coupe X, a Mercedes Mclaren SLR and SL65 Black series, the Lamborghini Murcielago, Gallardo and Diablo as well as the Pontiac GTO Firebird and Ferrari 360 Modena.

Sharing the garage were Lolly's motorbikes and a toy-car collection arranged on shelves running the entire length of the place. Next to his bar was the biggest slot car set-up I'd ever seen. The walls were decorated with murals of Kyalami, Monza, Route 66 and, beside the huge roller door, was a scene of New York City from the Brooklyn Bridge. In the distance were the Twin Towers, still standing majestically. When I first saw this art work, Lolly laughed and pointed out a Boeing, that he'd painted on himself, flying straight for the buildings.

Although he had fun collecting and driving exotic cars and bikes, which often brought out an almost boyish side in him (he enjoyed driving the symbols of his success), Robyn remembers him as moody and desperately lonely towards the end of his life. He would, on occasion, call Robyn and Ricardo into work over weekends or public holidays. Once they arrived, Lolly would conveniently 'forget' what it was he needed them to do and take them out for lunch instead. The source of Lolly's wretchedness was difficult to identify but may, in part, have included his failing marriage and difficult relationships with his children. Trying to escape his unhappiness, he threw himself into distractions like poker, which was one of the few things that seemed to make him genuinely happy.

One day Lolly walked into the office and told us he'd won an Aprilia superbike the night before while playing poker. Anticipating a story, Ricardo, Robyn and I stopped what we were doing and sat up to listen.

With a delighted smile, Lolly told us that he and a friend, Ari Psaltis, had become bored towards the end of the poker game that was being played in the monstrous garage at Lolly's Kyalami house, and they decided to have some fun. They each took a poker chip in hand and wagered that the person who could throw the chip the closest to the huge roll-up garage door would win one of the other's motorbikes. Ari would, if he won, take ownership of Lolly's Ducati and Lolly would (should he win) claim Ari's Aprilia.

Ari threw first and, as Lolly recounted the story, I could

imagine the chip flying through the air, down the middle of the garage, zooming past the supercar collection to its right and left. He told us he was having heart failure as he saw that it was going to land right at the door, but then fate intervened and the chip flipped up and began to roll on its side. Eventually, Ari's chip ended up hitting the garage door and rolling back a few metres, giving Lolly the gap he needed to win the bounty.

Lolly threw and the chip ended up sliding neatly along the black-tiled floor, and eventually wedged under the door itself. I have a feeling that at some point before this bet was made, Lolly had spent time practising – hence the idea to throw a poker chip at the garage door.

The next day Lolly's bank manager from First National Bank, Mike Hatton-Jones, arrived at the Rivonia office to chat and Lolly persuaded Mike to give him a lift so he could ride back on the bike he'd won. Before they left, Lolly managed to scrounge an old bucket helmet and grabbed a pair of oversized sunglasses that had been left in the office by a dancer. I can imagine people's response to seeing Lolly ride past, straddling his newly acquired superbike and looking ridiculous in his 'riding gear'.

At this point, Lolly's working days started with getting business dealings out of the way as soon as possible so that he could escape into the world of poker. So great was Lolly's need for distraction, he'd often play into the early hours of the morning and later pass out from exhaustion at his desk. Robyn says that while Lolly's mood improved towards the end, he still exuded a great sense of sadness.

Needing to prepare themselves for Lolly's legendary mood swings, Teazers' employees had developed a fail-safe way of assessing Lolly's emotional state – his choice of cars. If Lolly arrived in his yellow Ferrari or green Lamborghini (nicknamed 'The Hulk'), this spelt trouble. Instead, they prayed to see the remarkable Koenigsegg, its trumpeting exhaust pipes announcing the arrival of Lolly's playful *alter ego*.

Ultimately, cars and poker were Lolly's favourite pastimes. These were simple pleasures, unlike the tax-evading juggernaut that was Teazers, and the complexities of the fairer sex. Behind the wheel or with a hand of cards he'd been dealt, Lolly felt in control. These were vehicles for his self-indulgence. After all, what was the point of being the King of Teaze if not to enjoy the fruits of hedonism?

3
WORKING FOR THE LOLLY

I joined Teazers in May 2009 after the economic downturn put an end to my career as an IT project manager. My fiancée, Samantha, had also just fallen pregnant. If I was to be a father, I was determined not to be an unemployed one.

While hosting our engagement party at Teazers a few months earlier, I made the acquaintance of Lolly's PA, Robyn. Jobless and frantic I later called her in the desperate hope that there might be a managerial position opening at Teazers. She kindly offered to ensure that my CV would be at the top of the pile when a vacancy cropped up.

While I might have fooled myself into believing that I enjoyed working in the IT industry, it was just a means to an end – this was something I could do while I searched for a job I could be passionate about. Like my own father, I'm an unconventional person who likes being outspoken.

The appeal of working at Teazers had very little to do with the actual strip club itself (not that the 'office scenery' hurt), but centred primarily around working with Lolly Jackson. I had devoured all the information I could find regarding the man and his escapades and felt a strong connection with him. While the possibility of learning from his entrepreneurial skills was a draw-card, I think I was also attracted to his non-conformist persona. The fact that my wife had worked in the massage industry for years also made me curious to learn more about the business.

I can still vividly remember the telephone call in May when I was told to be at the Teazers Rivonia offices the following Monday at 11.00 am. The weekend passed agonisingly slowly, not only because I was broke, but also because I was intimidated by the prospect of meeting Lolly Jackson face to face. I'd always admired his ingenuity; he'd spotted a gap in the market and then vigorously exploited it. In my mind, he was larger than life and cut an impressive figure. Walking nervously into Teazers, I knew that this interview could lead to a unique opportunity to learn at the feet of a master – a man who had barely received an education, but who'd created an empire.

Located off the reception area of the club and up a steep flight of stairs was an area where Ricardo and Robyn were seated (*see Appendix 1 on page 221*). The two of them chatted while another candidate and I waited nervously outside Lolly's office. My anxiety increased when Lolly's booming voice burst through the open door. Clearly, some of his managers had disappointed him and I made a mental note never to put myself in that unenviable position. Even though my days of public speaking and debating at school had taught me to embrace my fear, that morning it took every ounce of self-restraint I could muster to keep from running out the door.

Once Lolly had finished neutering his staff, he dismissed them and ordered us in. 'I don't have time for this crap. Both of you – come in together,' he barked. I soon realised that Lolly was going to pit us against each other as a test to see who wanted the job the most. He started by asking my fellow candidate about his previous employment. The gentleman bleakly explained that he'd held a management position with a bank but had lost his job as a result of cutbacks. His tale painted a woeful picture of a constant struggle to make ends meet while his wife, who the bank had fortunately kept on, supported them.

Lolly went on to ask the man about his family. He then turned to me and followed the same line of questioning, finally asking me how I thought my fiancée would react to her husband-to-be being surrounded by naked women all day. I briefly explained that Samantha had worked in the massage industry for years and that this had helped to forge a strong, trusting bond between us.

Lolly nodded, turned to the other candidate and delivered his verdict. He felt that the man's age was a drawback and that the dignity of his family could become compromised by his working at a strip club. He added that, judging by what the man had told him about his family, working at Teazers would only be a temporary fix and not a lasting solution.

I then became the object of Lolly's steely gaze as he asked for my CV. He studied the papers dispassionately, raised his head and, with reference to my public speaking and debating, asked if I was any good. I told him I'd reached SA Schools' level and could hold my own.

My so-called 'raw talent' was identified by my English teacher Andrea Graham at Jeppe Boys, who also pushed me to work harder at achieving better grades. Even when I went to St Andrew's School in Bloemfontein, my new-found passion was picked up by my English teacher Kerry Gower. She suggested I try my hand at debating.

Two years later, I was promoted to second speaker on our first team and we qualified to compete in SA Schools. I've always enjoyed engaging in verbal battle and had no idea this skill would cement my later career.

Next, Lolly asked about my web design work and enquired whether I could manage stock control on a computer. I said that I could, making a mental note to do some extra research on this subject if I got the job. Finally, he simply said that I should come back the following day at 8.00 am. From that point on, I was officially employed by Lolly Jackson. The salary he offered was a paltry R10 000 pm, but I accepted it immediately.

When I joined Teazers, Ricardo saw me as someone who could take over the mundane, frustrating tasks he hated, such as ordering stock, stock retrieval and managing the day-to-day operations of the Rivonia branch. Personally, I felt that he shouldn't have had to deal with such trivialities in the first place.

I started off stock-taking by day and undergoing two hours of management training each night. Lolly was absent quite a bit as he was renovating his house in Kyalami. When he did come to work, it was to pay the dancers and sign cheques. Ricardo helped Lolly with these tasks and I soon came to realise that the staff were more than merely colleagues working for the same company – this was a close-knit family. Lolly was pedantic about enforcing certain rules of conduct among his staff. While some protested at these strict boundaries, they nonetheless served a purpose in creating the fantasy he was selling.

Lolly insisted on things like nails being neatly manicured at all times. He was a stickler regarding this point as he felt that no man wanted to see chipped and bitten nails. He always emphasised 'Be a fantasy, not a reality', and never sleep with clients. Any dancer who picked up weight went onto the 'Fat Butt' list, which meant they'd have to pay a levy until Lolly was satisfied. The girls would only be allowed to eat the slimmer's meal of the day. Dancers had to be polite, courteous and friendly – everything the customer's wife was not – at all times. If there was a problem, then the manager or Lolly himself would attend to it. Unless booked for an extended period of time, each dancer had five songs to get to know the customer and ask politely if he wanted a dance. If he replied 'no', the dancer had to move on to make way for the next girl.

The dancers who took issue with Lolly's management style were the same ones who continually broke the rules. While I agree that some of these regulations were a bit harsh, it was nonetheless Lolly's business and the conduct of the girls reflected on him as the owner. Customers knew the drill as well as the girls did – no touching, no propositioning and no drugs. Patrons were also not allowed to walk around from table to table so as to save on paying for their own dances.

Three weeks into my internship, Ricardo got a call from Lolly saying I was to move across to the Midrand branch as a manager. I was devastated; I could feel my opportunity to learn from Lolly slipping away. After only three days at my new job, I called Ricardo and begged him to speak to Lolly on my behalf. The intervention worked and Lolly drove out to Midrand so that we could talk to each other in person.

As he arrived, reception flicked the waitress lights repeatedly to alert everyone, and the club snapped to attention. Lolly walked around barking orders and then pulled me aside. With his usual directness, he asked why I was so adamant about remaining at the Rivonia office. I told him my reasons and he then asked how badly I wanted to do this. (I would learn in time that tests were a way of life for Lolly.) I drove home the point that I wanted to learn from him, which he accepted, but he told me such a thing would come at a price: 'I can't pay you a manager's salary, so you will have to take a cut down to R7 000.' I agreed and shook his hand enthusiastically. I have never been sure whether he was just trying to save money or was pleased he'd found someone willing to take a risk to get what they wanted.

The first project I took on after moving back to the Rivonia office was putting together a Teazers' calendar. I suggested the idea to Lolly, explaining that as we had both desirable cars and beautiful women on hand, it would be relatively simple to pull together. He mulled over the idea and then in typical Lolly style, proclaimed we'd produce not a 12- but a 24-month calendar. Lolly always had to go bigger and better.

After we'd finished compiling the calendar, I emailed Lolly the final print-ready layout. True to form, he immediately emailed it to five of his friends, bragging about this achievement. They, in turn, emailed it to their friends. I'd no idea it had gone viral until Stuart Williams, the photographer responsible for the shoot, called to say he'd received 'a copy' via email from a staff member in the motoring section at *The Star* who had said he really liked his photographs! Lolly good-naturedly laughed it off, claiming it was free advertising, but he did later wonder why he was unable to recover the R100 000 printing cost. To this day, despite many copies having been enthusiastically bought, a stack of calendars still sits in the Teazers Rivonia storeroom; most of our potential customers had already received their emailed copy for free.

I savoured those rare moments working on the calendar with Lolly, but it was during this time that he would often pass disturbing comments such as, 'I've lost my passion for this business and need to find it again.' Initially, I thought this was the stress talking, but time revealed that these statements spoke of some greater inner conflict. I had my own demons to contend with at that time – primarily in the form of my financial woes. However, the fact that I loved my job helped – I just hadn't found my niche in the business yet. The last week of September would see me discovering what I wanted to do.

Lolly had conceptualised a publicity stunt a month earlier – brilliantly focused on the then-current gender-testing debate raging on in SA athletics. Although we would never have admitted it at the time, Caster Semenya (the athlete embroiled in a gender-testing farce in 2009) was the subject of our plan to inflame the public and encourage media attention. On Monday 28 September an email from the Advertising Standards Authority (ASA) arrived at our offices. Just one week prior, we'd erected a billboard on Rivonia Road showing a semi-nude woman accompanied by the payoff line: 'No need for gender testing.'

The ASA said two complaints (*see Appendix 2 on page 222*) had been registered with them and we needed to provide them with a copy of the offending billboard artwork, along with any comments in response. This was usually Robyn's responsibility, but she was inundated with work so I offered to draft the letter for her. After some initial resistance, Lolly agreed and I set to work.

The letter was written in my most sarcastic tone and, over the course of three pages, I drove home the point that the model wasn't actually naked; she was, in fact, wearing very expensive shoes (*see Appendix 3 on page 225*). Lolly examined what I'd produced and, once satisfied, told me, 'Well done my boy – send it.'

By the following afternoon, the advert had stirred up international interest. It also initiated what would become a ritual for Lolly and me. Each time Teazers made the news, I'd get a call in the morning telling me to buy copies of all the newspapers and read each article to him while he was still in bed (Lolly would quickly lose interest if he or Teazers weren't on the front page). We'd then devise a strategy on how to maximise publicity.

Lolly went on the offensive, blaming the ASA for escalating the public's interest in the topic, and stubbornly refused to admit that there was any link between the advert and Caster Semenya.

While this media storm was brewing, my home life had taken a turn for the worse. Samantha and I had been arguing heatedly for some time and she had temporarily moved in with her father, a fact that I happened to mention to Ricardo. Soon enough, I was summoned into Lolly's office. He asked me why I hadn't told him that my fiancée was no longer living with me. I replied that I regarded work and home life as two separate entities, and at this stage in my career I couldn't afford to allow my domestic situation to distract me from my work. He nodded sagely and told me I could go, adding, 'My boy, they always come back. Don't worry, they always come back.'

By the Wednesday, it seemed the hype surrounding the controversial advert was beginning to die down, which was not what we wanted. I called Lolly and told him I'd found out that the ANC Youth League were planning to donate some money to Caster in recognition of her athletic achievements. I suggested we do the same and use it to our advantage. He asked how much I thought we should give her. I said R10 000 and he, typically, shot back with R20 000.

The next day Lolly stopped in at the office. He handed me a blank cheque and told me to find out who to pay it to and to make sure it was delivered immediately – ensuring, of course, that the media was alerted to what was happening (*see Appendix 4 on page 230*). Later Ricardo told me that Lolly had increased my monthly salary by R1 000; a recognition of my efforts. The week came to an end with Lolly telling me that from then on I'd be handling his press releases and compiling his business letters. This was my first lesson in the power of controversy. We'd taken a simple low-cost billboard and used it as a very effective publicity stunt that had attracted worldwide media attention.

A short while after the Caster Semenya billboard controversy, Lolly came up with the idea that we should send a message to the ASA. Excitedly, he told me to get hold of Stuart Williams, the photographer we'd used for the calendar, and set up some shots of Demi. His brief was that she should look like a secretary, complete with glasses, which she'd be pushing up the bridge of her nose with her middle finger. Not deliberately of course.

Demi was far from charmed by the idea. She hated the thought of being vilified by upsetting the public even further. Her concerns were justified as Lolly planned to use, as a background to the shot, none other than an image of the previous billboard with the words 'ASA banned' splashed across it. Despite Demi's reservations, Lolly got his way – as usual. Interestingly, there were no come-backs as the ASA had clearly understood this was a blatant attempt at further publicity. Lolly even went so far as to have his friends register complaints, but the ASA refused to take the bait.

After this incident, it became Lolly's practice to dictate letters, pacing the office floor while ranting, a diatribe which I then had to transcribe, edit and package. Topics would vary, but the same expression would always crop up: 'You's fucking clowns.' This was Lolly's trademark statement. The letters went out to plastic surgeons who refused to operate until Lolly's cheques had cleared, lawyers he felt charged too much for their services and persons I'd tracked down who Lolly held personally responsible for potholes in the roads. No one was spared. I felt honoured that Lolly trusted me to be his voice.

In November 2009, we got an email from law firm Adams and Adams complaining of copyright infringement. They demanded that our billboard with the line 'Kyk Net' be instantly removed. Failure to do so would result in immediate legal action.

As usual, I called the press and told them about the complaint. Lolly explained it by saying all he did was to use a simple term that meant 'Just Look' in Afrikaans. He asked cheekily if he'd be sued by OK and Checkers if he ran the line, 'Teazers is OK, come check it out.' I thought all this was brilliant until I googled the location of the billboard – it was situated on a corner beside the Multichoice building! (KykNET is, of course, a television channel owned by Multichoice). When this was pointed out, Lolly roared with laughter, shrugged his shoulders and gave instructions to take it down. Free publicity always managed to improve his mood.

On another occasion, the Sandton sheriff arrived at our head office with a truck looking for movable assets to cover the cost of a judgment. Lolly flew through to the office to accost the poor government official and delivered a string of abuse at him. When the sheriff dared to say that Lolly shouldn't speak to him like that, Lolly's teetering attempts at self-restraint lost traction. He kicked his desk, punched a family picture hanging near his door and then turned his anger on a stainless-steel dustbin. He kicked it so hard it ended up looking like an hourglass.

After Lolly's rage had subsided, he looked again at the summons, and realised it had been made out to one of the many companies that owned no assets! Gleefully, he turned to Ricardo and ordered him to give the sheriff a stapler and that he should write down exactly how many staples were in it. The sheriff saw that this was a losing battle and, after getting the necessary documents signed, got the hell out of there.

After the man left, Lolly pinched the dustbin from our office to replace his battered one. While still skulking around, muttering under his voice, I thought I'd crack a joke and said, 'Boss, the bin is taking you to the CCMA.' The look on his face was priceless – a mixture of agitation and confusion. 'What the hell are you on about?' he screamed. My expression as deadpan as I could muster, I said, 'It got canned,' which provoked near-hysterical laughter.

Lolly's habits were legendary and they gave us a way in which to have some fun at his expense. Among my favourites was his tendency to trip on the rail at the front door. He'd grumble some expletives before bellowing for Robyn to come down and empty the 'drop safe' area, and it became a game for me to guess whether I could pre-empt his habitual bellow by calling Robyn in my best 'Lolly voice'. On the occasions I got it right, we'd all collapse laughing while he'd scream, 'What are you's fucking clowns laughing at?' which would send us into even greater fits of laughter – Lolly not realising that everyone was laughing at my impersonation rather than his having tripped over the rail.

One particular Monday, Ricardo and Robyn wanted to leave work at 4.00 pm, so we devised a plan. Our idea was to amuse Lolly so he'd reward us and send us home early. I sent him an SMS saying, 'Dear boss. The slaves wish to remind you that today is National Slave Day. We would deeply appreciate the chance to go home at four to celebrate with our families.' No one expected me to actually send it, and Robyn and Ricardo went pale when they heard Lolly's cellphone pinging in his office. After a moment we heard him yell, 'Slaves aren't traded, they're sold!' after which he laughed and told us to go.

If we wanted peace and quiet on a Friday, we'd simply remind him that the courts were closing soon and he should head for the hills unless he wanted to spend the weekend in prison. This inevitably worked as Lolly had been arrested too many times on a Friday, and hated spending the weekend in a holding cell.

True to Lolly's words, Samantha and I got back together, but by October 2009 my financial problems had escalated to the point that I was on the brink of losing everything. Desperation taking hold, I swallowed my pride and asked Lolly for help. The next day he called me into his office and showed me a map he'd drawn with directions to a house his dancers had lived in in Bedfordview. It had been standing virtually empty since a fire had ravaged it and, since my wife had owned and worked in a massage parlour, he suggested we set up a similar business in these premises.

He gave me the next day off so my family and I could move to the Bedfordview house from where we would operate the business and he paid me an advance on my salary. When I asked whether he'd consider a loan to kick-start the business, Lolly said no, saying that if I was given things in life, I wouldn't appreciate them. He added that if people had to fight for success and had no other option, they would succeed. If I could learn this lesson, he would reward me.

By February 2010, I was paying Lolly rent and at this stage he asked to inspect the business. When he got back to the office, he asked me to join him and shut the door. He said nothing for a while, prolonging my agony, and then smiled and said he was proud of me. He had similar plans for the garages downstairs at the Teazers Rivonia branch and, a week later, arrived with the builders' drawings. I was incredibly excited – Lolly and I were in business together and it looked as if I had a bright future.

During this time I felt close and safe enough with Lolly to approach him about something highly personal. I'd tried to speak with him privately for some time without success and, just before my daughter Alexis's birth, on 4 February 2010, I saw my boss playing poker alone in his office. Lolly's poker time was sacrosanct, so I nervously asked if I could speak with him and he nodded in agreement.

I opened with the line that what I was about to say had nothing to do with money; it was personal. I explained that Samantha and I felt that he'd saved our lives and that we were very grateful for the help he had given us at a time when we needed it the most. He said, 'My boy, I saved *your* life not hers; she was going to kill you!' That statement broke the tension but I needed to finish what I had started.

I told him I'd understand if he felt I was crossing a line. Seeing his poker game being jeopardised, he asked me to get to the point. I blurted out that it would be an honour and a privilege if he'd accept the role of godfather to my child. Within moments he was on his feet, smiling broadly and shaking my hand, saying the honour and privilege would be all his.

I realised that my request could easily have been turned down and I was thrilled that it made him so happy. In 2009, Radovan had asked Lolly to be his son's godfather; however, he received an SMS only days before the christening, saying Radovan's mother felt this honour should be reserved for a family member. Lolly was devastated, swearing and slamming the door of his office, before retreating into an angry depression.

While working at Teazers might seem to have been all about pranks and pissing off the public and media, there was a darker side to the business, and indeed, to Lolly. While he mixed with notorious people daily, Lolly seemed particularly attracted to Radovan. Perhaps it was Lolly's ego and his competitive nature that saw him constantly vying with his friend. The two were renowned for racing their supercars at 300 km/h, with neither willing to give in – even at the risk of losing their lives. Where there's similarity, there's bound to be rivalry.

4
MASTERS AND SERVANTS

Lolly Jackson was a remarkably complex character. Those who knew him describe Lolly as the epitome of youthful exuberance. Also known for his violent mood swings that would instantly transform him from sensitive man to raging beast, he was passionate, creative, abrasive, egotistical, ambitious, self-centred, generous and caring.

January 2010 began like any other month. On our first day back at work after the December holidays, we settled in quickly, driven by our relentless taskmaster. It was the year of South Africa's hosting of the Soccer World Cup, and it was hoped that our country and companies were going to shine. Lolly was brimming with ideas on how to make the most of the expected influx of tourists and had, at that stage, already been interviewed by a Mexican television station. He'd also managed to convince the tour operators from that hot, sultry country that they should bring their groups to our clubs for some light-hearted adult entertainment.

He began to conceptualise a voucher system designed to lure customers with discounted rates and specials. Despite all these carefully laid marketing traps, we were instructed not to raise our prices one iota. In fact, we actually reduced the rates! This strategy was cleverly thought through as we didn't want to alienate our local patrons whose continued support we would need once our visitors had left. Lolly's maxim was 'show them a good time at a good price and they'll keep coming back' – his business acumen proved sound as the figures would later reveal.

In my view, Lolly managed to challenge the preconception that the adult entertainment industry was a seedy, questionable one that yielded profits in exchange for little or no effort. What has often been ignored is that Lolly was first and foremost a businessman. And a talented one at that, who had run a number of highly successful operations (despite somewhat dubious methods) – where others involved in similar businesses had failed or had only scratched the surface of possibility.

Robyn uncovered a blog one day via a Google Alert entitled, *A small business lesson from Lolly Jackson (scan QR code 2 on page 218)*. It praised Lolly for being a forerunner as a brand strategist and business guru, and he could hardly contain his joy as he devoured the piece. Literally beaming, he made us print it out.

His enjoyment of this recognition was short-lived and as we assembled for a staff meeting, Lolly quickly reverted to his usual self, swearing and belligerent. He emphatically urged us to increase our efforts in the business – a tirade seemingly fuelled by the online acclaim he'd received. He had a vision for the year to come and was at pains to encourage us in his own special way.

The dancers were the first to receive his unwelcome attention. Lolly said that the next time he caught one of them fucking his clients, he'd drag the unfortunate Lothario on stage and beat him to within an inch of his life. This was a clear allusion to the Michael Kalymnios case, as a result of which Lolly had received defamation-of-character summonses totalling over R5 million. According to Lolly, this was a farce because, as far as he was concerned, he had only ever spoken the truth. (Lolly had called the former Teazers' dancer Yuliyana Moshorovs'ka – with whom Michael had ostensibly become romantically involved – a 'whore' and Teazers' client Michael a 'fat fuck'.)

Continuing his tirade, Lolly spat out that if the dancers didn't like the way he was running things, they could 'stand up right now and fuck off to The Grand. The grass is only greener on the other side because more people are shitting there.' This was Soccer World Cup year, and it seemed that nothing was going to stand in his way. Lolly asked me to join him at the top of the staircase from which he held court over the entire Gauteng group's staff and dancers. He asked that I re-read the blog to them. I'd begun – feeling like a medieval town crier – when he abruptly stopped me. 'Read it slower,' he said, 'the dancers don't understand English to begin with; damn foreigners.'

After dismissing the dancers, Lolly turned his ire on the permanent staff. He said that he felt we were simply going through the motions, and demanded that our passion return right now. 'Stop getting a salary and start earning one!' he shouted. He said that he expected all of us to live the Teazers' brand and encouraged us to use our initiative – a far cry from the *modus operandi* of those soul-destroying corporates that only wanted soldier ants. Despite the salary structure leaving much to be desired, Lolly told us that we were fortunate to have employment at all, given the economic climate, and he was going to squeeze every last drop of effort out of us.

Next in line were the DJs. Having been a DJ himself, this particular occupation was one that was dear to Lolly's heart, however it also meant that the disc jockeys often got the worst of it. Many a time we'd hear Lolly screaming from his office, telling Robyn to get a dancer to change her routine as he despised one (or all) of her songs. He was particular about the music played in the clubs and often hated the tracks the DJs chose. Even though he relented over 'house' music, he had an addendum, of course: 'The first time I catch some fuck making boxes with his hands in aisle-ways, I am going to fuck you all up.' I nearly burst out laughing as the impassioned Lolly emphasised his statement with wild hand gestures (referencing how ravers dance) – hands that could easily turn into fists if I wasn't careful!

Lolly's staff meetings never failed to fascinate me. Ricardo, Robyn and I would sit on the sidelines, taking notes and keeping outside the direct line of fire. We watched entranced as Lolly delivered his sermon; pausing only from time to time for a sip of water. The master was at work and we were his receptive disciples – eager to take in the wisdom he had to offer.

By the end of January, Lolly's World Cup mania seemed to subside. He was also exhibiting a new-found awareness of financial prudence and was counting the cents – something he'd never done before. He asked me to send letters to the bank, threatening to close his cheque accounts as a result of the bank's failure to pay interest on positive balances even though this was in fact standard policy. Lolly was determined, but eventually had to settle on the compromise of a money-market account on the side. For the first time in years, we were told to buy alcohol via direct suppliers. Even though it would tie up hundreds of thousands of rands, the satisfaction of saving a few thousand now made sense to him. He explained this new-found financial zeal by telling us that he'd been overlooked for an incentive tour offered by Jägermeister and that this was unacceptable.

Lolly's appetite for money saw him entering into agreements that allowed sports betting at all Teazers' venues during the World Cup, this on the understanding that he receive a decent cut of the profits. But despite his multilayered talents and his vibrant, innovative and fun-loving personality, in the weeks preceding his death, this outspoken and demonstrative man had become withdrawn and sullen. It would soon become evident that the Lolly Jackson we knew was about to be defeated.

5
BREAKDOWN

After our daughter Alexis was born on 12 February 2010, Sam and I decided it was time to make things 'official'. We agreed to get married at home in a quiet, intimate ceremony on the 28th. I was given the task of inviting close friends and family but when I tried calling Lolly on his various phones there was no answer. Becoming increasingly concerned, I tried to reach him by calling Demi. The phone rang for a long time and when she eventually answered, all I could hear were howls of anguish. Demi was sobbing so hard she was literally gasping for breath. I could barely make out her words, but I soon realised what she was saying: Lolly was leaving her!

I asked her what was going on and she repeated that it was over; she'd initiated a split and Lolly would be moving to their holiday home in Westlake Estate, Hartbeespoort Dam. I tried in vain to console her and recall slumping on the couch after the conversation had ended, saying to Sam that I was worried about what impact this would have on all of our lives. For the next few days, I regularly called Demi to see how she was coping. She said she was tired of the way Lolly treated her – the abuse, the late nights and the constant affairs – and had reached her watershed moment.

Nichol Fabre later told Karyn Maughan after Lolly's death that 'Lolly didn't speak to her [Demi] properly' and that 'the last two years of her relationship were terrible. When he started playing poker, he was hardly at home. I know they lived apart for a couple of weeks before he died. She said that she still loved him, but wanted to be happy. She said she was sick and tired of the girls at Teazers and how they influenced her relationship.' (*scan QR code 3 on page 218 to listen to this interview*)

My heart went out to Demi who had so courageously and defiantly said 'no more'. There was no denying that Lolly was a difficult character, but I was haunted by images of him dying alone – a sentiment that proved unhappily prophetic.

Lolly's routine had now changed. He'd go from work to his Kyalami house to change cars and then leave for Hartbeespoort Dam. The next morning, the cycle was repeated in reverse.

In typical Lolly style he arranged a distraction from his woes in the form of a boat party, with Radovan, other friends and strippers in attendance on the day of our nuptials. He'd forgotten all about the wedding, but when Robyn reminded him, he told me he'd definitely make it.

On the night before my wedding, I went to the kitchen to get a beer and came back to find a number of missed calls on my cellphone from Teazers Rivonia and Lolly's personal mobile number. Concerned, I quickly called him back. 'My boy, my boy – call the press! Get them in play, I'm being arrested,' he burbled. I asked if he'd called his lawyer and Lolly said 'yes', and that the police were taking him to Johannesburg Central Police Station (John Vorster Square). It then emerged that Lolly's arrest followed charges of intimidation and extortion laid by Michael Kalymnios.

Outside the station, I met up with Radovan and Jerome Safi, who was an employee of Krejcir. Both men had tried without success to see Lolly, but he'd been placed in the high-risk section of the station and only lawyers and investigating officers were allowed in.

After speaking with Ian Jordaan, Lolly's lawyer, who was holding Lolly's belt and shoelaces, I realised there was little more we could do. I went home after releasing a statement to the press and was in contact with Lolly during my wedding, as Ian had slipped him a cellphone during their morning consultation. Did it disturb Sam or me that Lolly couldn't make it to our wedding? No – we were concerned with his well-being, and understood his predicament. There had been no malicious intent from his side and I certainly didn't envy him sitting in a dank cell while life outside continued.

Whereas, ordinarily, Lolly would have leant on Demi for support, this time he called on Ricardo and myself. We talked throughout the weekend before his Monday court appearance. Demi later told me that while she felt sympathy for her husband during this time, she wouldn't allow this incident to cause her to give in. However, in an effort to help, she and Ricardo cleared the safes at the Midrand and Rivonia clubs so that I could pay Lolly's bail the following day.

◉

After he was released, Lolly's attitude towards Demi changed dramatically. He would shift between attempts at placation and kindness, and bombarding his wife with expletives and threats. Demi tried to be amicable, but she insisted that any possible reconciliation had to be on her terms. She demanded of Lolly that he give up Teazers and commit himself solely to her (Demi confessed this to me as well as to other people), but she agreed to maintain the mantle of the 'good wife' – which meant that Lolly could still enjoy certain benefits.

Demi later admitted to me that, in an effort to strike a compromise with Lolly regarding his clandestine philandering, she had devised a strategy where if there was any bedroom action to be had, it would be under her control and she needed to be included. However, the group-sex activities she arranged for the two of them seemed only to confuse Lolly further and he'd say to Ricardo, 'Where do I draw the line? She wants me to bring women home, but I'm not allowed to be with other women?'

And there were lots of other women. According to Nichol, before I started working at Teazers Lolly was involved in an affair with a dancer named Jane, but 'it was more than a one-night stand; he had feelings for her. Demi found an SMS on his phone where Jane had taken a naked pic of herself in the shower.' (*scan QR code 4 on page 218 to listen to this interview*)

Jane was sent back to Bulgaria where, according to Ricardo, she gave birth to a child – the father of whom is unknown (Robyn alleges that Jane had had an abortion). It is clear though that the affair had caused an irreparable rift in the marriage and had spawned several vicious arguments.

Ricardo recalls one occasion: 'He [Lolly] came in from

lunch and said to me, "Get out the Pty Ltd cheque book and write the bitch [Demi] out a cheque for R2 million",' in front of a distraught Demi. Ricardo adds that, two years later, 'Demi found out that Lolly was still seeing Jane after she [Jane] went home [to Bulgaria]. I think that was the last straw for Demi. Lolly had cash slips in his pocket which he usually gave to me, but this time he didn't pass them over and Demi found the receipts for two people at a hotel in Greece. Lolly excused them saying, "It was Sarios and me." But Demi phoned the hotel and they confirmed that it was for a Mr and Mrs Jackson.' (*scan QR code 5 on page 218 to listen to this interview*)

When interviewed about her relationship with Lolly, Demi said, while she loved him very much, she knew he was cheating on her, and this exerted an enormous toll on their relationship. Demi tells the story of how Lolly asked Jane to impersonate her (Demi) at a Greek bank to open a joint account (in his and Demi's name), an account Demi insists she knew nothing about. She also said that Lolly had used this account for money laundering which resulted in Demi being investigated for her apparent involvement.

Demi confirms that she found the hotel receipts, but maintains she chose not to confront Lolly with the information she had discovered from the hotel, because he'd previously told her that 'the people who accuse other people are the ones that are doing things themselves'.

I'd learnt of one of Lolly's 'extracurricular' activities with a 20-year-old Bulgarian dancer named Dani as a result of a television show we were involved with for *Ignition TV*. The programme was being filmed in Lolly's garage at his Kyalami house and Dani was cast as a model. The crew told me that shooting wrapped up at 12.00 pm, but Dani was only collected at 3.00 pm that afternoon. At the risk of sounding sexist, Dani wasn't exactly a budding conversationalist and we all understood the nature of this extended visit.

In an interview with Karyn Maughan, Demi insisted she never cheated on Lolly. 'I moved out two months before Lolly was murdered... I was tired, tired of Lolly fucking me around six-love, he was always messing me around... I was tired of the lying and being alone all the time. I woke at six o'clock in the morning so I could clean the house and cut the lawn because I didn't have domestic help. Lolly would take me out for supper once in a while. After his death, I found out he was taking all these different girls out for supper.'

Demi knew Lolly was seeing an international model. 'The one night they went out and he left her so that he could look for me. She sent him an SMS promising to show him a good time if he came back... I did her eyebrows for free at my salon. I didn't know it, but I was making her beautiful for him!

'I remember after I told him I was leaving, he came into my bedroom and said to me, "Look me in the eye and tell me you want a divorce"... And I said yes, this is what I want. He tore up our wedding album after that.'

With problems between Lolly and Demi escalating, Lolly withdrew more and more into his world of gambling.

While Lolly was out of town playing in a poker tournament in February 2010, Demi had to come into the office to sign cheques on her husband's behalf. She was sitting in Lolly's office when Dani, the dancer from the *Ignition* shoot, sauntered through the door. Demi lost her temper, hurling abuse at the dancer, and then demanded Ricardo fine the girl R5 000 for 'acting like she owned the place'. Ricardo simply took the path of least resistance and headed quickly back to the change rooms. Still shaken by this encounter, Demi later went upstairs to La Diva – a beauty salon she once owned – and sat with its new owner Claudia, a former dancer named Madison, and Robyn. As I was about to leave work, I was asked to come upstairs with a bottle of wine and a sealed bottle of Patrón, and Demi spent the night drinking away her sorrows.

The following Tuesday, Lolly and Demi's relationship apparently reached the point of no return. Lolly told me afterwards, referring to the 'condom incident', how he and Demi had gone out for lunch that day and that things seemed to be going well. He then suggested to her, with a glint in his eye, that they go home and 'make things right'. While Demi accepted, she said they could have sex only if Lolly wore a condom.

The day before, unknown to me, Robyn had told Lolly that Demi was seeing her high-school sweetheart, Tyrel Manson. Now, taken aback by Demi's condom conditions, and feeling shocked by her hypocrisy, Lolly's temper raged out of control. Back in our offices Lolly screamed, 'Is she suggesting that I'm a dirty, diseased fucker who's going to give her precious little cunt something to take back to that dumb fuck she's screwing?' Lolly began barking orders. Policies were to be changed immediately and Demi was to be removed as a beneficiary; all funds were to be donated to the SPCA. Robyn and Ricardo began working feverishly as Lolly reasoned, 'At least those dogs still love you, no matter what.'

Robyn's task was to contact Econorisk and find out the procedure for removing Demi as a member of the family's medical aid, while Ricardo removed Demi's name from the insurance policies. I tried my best to disappear into the background while this tempest raged around me. Lolly kept popping in and out of his office mumbling, 'Who the fuck does she think she is?' while issuing decrees to his assistants. Demi's access to the Teazers' petrol account was terminated and her cellphone contract was cancelled. 'It's time to show the little bitch who's boss,' Lolly grumbled.

While Robyn and Ricardo were scrambling to complete these tasks, Lolly called his handyman, Lacksom, demanding he come directly to the office. On arrival, Lolly began shouting that he was not to call 'that bitch [Demi] "mammy" any more!' Lacksom protested at first, telling Lolly he was being unfair, but eventually he agreed. Ricardo was ordered to prepare an eviction letter, stating that Demi's mother had to move out of the Kloof Road house in Bedfordview immediately, and that Demi had until the end of the month to follow suit. Lolly signed this letter and handed it to Lacksom, who once again refused to follow orders. He eventually agreed after being told that if he didn't bring it back signed, he needn't come back at all. (A few days later, when Lolly had eventually calmed down, he actually withdrew the letter.)

Lolly instructed us to all 'unfriend' Demi on Facebook and told us that anyone caught communicating with her would be instantly fired.

Demi says Lolly told her he'd filed for divorce after she moved out of their Kyalami house in March 2010. Even though proceedings were underway, he kept calling and SMSing her, begging her to come back to him. 'He sent me an SMS saying he misses me, the monkeys miss me, I must come home,' she says. Demi asserts one of the hardest things about the break-up was leaving the pet monkeys they shared. 'Those monkeys were like my children... one of the monkeys was like my best friend. I hated leaving them.'

Demi claims she wanted to reconcile with Lolly and was in the process of moving back to their home when he was murdered. 'Now,' she says, 'I wish I'd divorced him. I got nothing from the will… I gave up a R10 million insurance payout so that we could pay SARS back. I sold my house on Kloof Road to pay SARS back. I have nothing now.'

6
FINAL DAYS

On the first day of March 2010, I realised just how vulnerable our once seemingly bulletproof leader was feeling. When he emerged from the holding cells of the Johannesburg Magistrates Court after being arrested in the Michael Kalymnios case, he looked ashen and drawn. Yet, true to form, Lolly attempted to mask his real feelings by offering me a wink and an utterance that everything would be OK.

Towards the end of the month, Lolly had had another dispute with his estranged wife. Apparently, he'd arrived at his Kyalami house to change cars, only to find that the locks on the doors, as well as all the security codes, had been changed. Lolly had evidently run riot, destroying objects and only stopping short of smashing a picture over Demi's head!

One afternoon that same month, my lift home got stuck in traffic and I found myself outside the Rivonia club with a disgruntled Lolly. Although reluctant at first to bring up the Demi issue, he clearly needed to unburden himself of the anger, sorrow, remorse and sense of failure he felt over the breakdown of his marriage. At one point during his outpouring he halted, thinking perhaps that he shouldn't be speaking so openly about his private life, concerned about his vulnerability. I said nothing but merely listened as Lolly continued to talk. That afternoon, I was offered a rare glimpse into his inner world. Lolly's anger was clearly directed towards Demi – both for not trusting him and for choosing to leave him. He knew, and admitted, that he had done wrong by her, but also felt he'd given her everything he possibly could. He loved her, he said, but was acutely aware that there was no going back. 'My boy, there are women out there that can do anything when it comes to business,' he lectured. 'Demi is not one of those. I've given her countless business opportunities and every time it's been a drain on my pocket. Some people are only good for cleaning houses.'

She was welcome to run off with this 'little dick' she'd found, he continued, but he would never fill Lolly's shoes. Lolly expounded at length about how high-maintenance Demi was, saying that the R2 million, car and house he was prepared to give her by way of a divorce settlement wouldn't go far. Then he spat out that she could 'go back to that shit-hole she'd crawled out of years ago and take her mom with her.' As the anger overwhelmed him, Lolly threatened to bash the old woman's teeth out – a justifiable act, he concluded, as he'd paid for the damn things.

Despite my efforts to calm him down, Lolly continued his harangue. He roared that Demi would have to find herself a job as her beau wouldn't be able to keep her in the manner to which she'd become accustomed. Eventually, his anger subsided as Manoli came out, offering his father a drink. The anger was now replaced with sadness. After Manoli went back inside, Lolly confessed, 'Do you know that Manoli told Demi I was cheating on her? Yes – how's that one? My own flesh and blood hates me so much he talks shit about me to her. Does he think he's going to inherit more if we get divorced? That's why I want to give it to the SPCA; at least those dogs still love you when you have nothing.' I was witnessing what felt like a spiritual purging and, as the sun was setting, we sat together on the wall outside the club and I listened to a deeply damaged man, a man who I nonetheless respected, as he gave voice to his demons.

The pain Lolly was feeling was palpable. He revealed that he believed he'd failed as a parent and that Manoli and Sam despised him. Their only concern, he said, was for his money. His sole hope lay in Julian who was still young enough to view his father as a hero.

His next revelation was startling: Lolly confessed that he was tired of the business and needed a change. His passion was gone and, if he was unable to rekindle it, he'd have to hand over the reins. He was tired of being the object of hatred and envy; the latter mostly felt by people 'too lazy to work for what they wanted'. Lolly complained that he received no credit for his efforts, despite having built a successful business empire. It seemed he wasn't good enough as the Teazers' business was part of the adult entertainment industry.

Despite his pride in his own achievements, Lolly told me that he felt that his failed marriage was undermining his years of hard work. He had been willing to try to change his ways and give it all up, but his window of opportunity had closed. Demi was in love with someone else. The world he operated in wasn't conducive to salvaging a marriage. If Lolly ever appeared to give preferential treatment to one dancer over another, even if his actions were merely dictated by his moods, rumours of infidelity would immediately start circulating. I confessed to him that I'd been concerned for his well-being and had spoken to Demi, who'd said that all she wanted was for her husband to treat her well and speak to her with respect. I added that he could fire me if he felt I had crossed a line, but I believed at the time that I had to speak to her about what was clearly a very troubling situation.

I suggested that perhaps Lolly should take some time off to reflect and take Demi away with him so they could talk things through. He conceded that this was sound advice, but replied that he was worried about leaving the business unattended. Regardless of anything I said to comfort him, Lolly just nodded and replied that perhaps it was time for things to come to an end.

Seeing that this avenue of discussion was closed, I made an attempt to lighten the mood. I told Lolly not to expect me to bring soup to his death bed as my hairy legs would look terrible in a nurse's uniform. This comment brought some welcome comic relief. Two days earlier, on 14 March 2010, Lolly had sent Ian Jordaan a simple SMS: 'Ian please go ahead with the divorce asap thx lolly.'

I remember thinking at the time what an irony it was that, to an outsider, Lolly seemed to have it all, but the truth was that he had nothing. Lolly's dark mood continued for days and we made a point of staying out of his way. During this time, Lolly avoided me as far as possible. It was almost as if he was embarrassed by having revealed his humanity to me, or perhaps he was expecting me to betray his confidence to Ricardo or Robyn. Writing this chapter is, in fact, the first time I've ever revealed the full details of our conversation.

In time, Lolly must have realised that his secrets were safe with me because he started to send me SMSs, joking that he was going to come for a massage at our venue. I told him I had his back to which he responded, 'I don't want *you* on my back, you clown. I want a beautiful woman.' He later sent another message stating that he knew what I meant and thanked me for listening.

Sadly, as the days wore on, Lolly began to care less about his work and threw himself instead into his beloved distraction, poker. He had grown morose and introverted, and his pervasive sense of doom seemed to be feeding on itself. Ex-wife Sharon was witness to this:

> 'I saw him exactly a month before he was killed: it was 3 April. I came up to Johannesburg as Julian was living with him and was meant to go spend the holidays with him. He phoned me before that and said Demi wasn't living with him and he couldn't look after Julian so I had to take him.
>
> 'Lolly then said, "Why don't you come for the weekend?" One of my friends was coming through, so I came up and I SMSed him from the airport to say, "Can we meet tomorrow to have lunch?" He said, "Yes, just give me a call tomorrow."
>
> 'We went to Monte Casino and at around lunch time I SMSed him again and said we were there and he should join us for a drink, and he said "On my way". I still have the SMS he sent me.
>
> 'We were sitting at an outside area that has couches when he came. We had a couple of drinks and were just talking shit, and I said to him that we'd booked to come back to that restaurant for supper. He said, "No, no, no – I want to take you to a Greek restaurant for supper."

'I said he didn't have to do that but he said he wanted to spend time with us. I could see he was lonely, so I agreed.

'He was quite jovial – although very reserved in the beginning – but we were talking about old times and he was telling me about his whole jail episode. It was while we were sitting talking that he said he had a hit on him. He knew he was going to die. His words to me were: "My murder will be another Brett Kebble case." He said that to my face, he knew he was a marked man.

'I still said to him, "Don't be ridiculous – you have like, nine lives." He just looked at me and said, "Well, everybody dies sometime."'

Lolly's premonition of his murder, and his linking the possibility to the death of the mining magnate, carried some weight as he knew all the parties involved in the Kebble case. When Brett was gunned down on 27 September 2005, Lolly had asked Robyn the next day to delete certain numbers from his phone: those of Brett Kebble and the man who would eventually admit to having pulled the trigger, Mikey Schultz. Lolly's request to have Mikey's number deleted from his phone was surprising as the two of them had been long-time friends. They even had matching superbikes and Mikey had been Lolly's best man at his wedding. The day after the Kebble murder, Lolly met with a member of the Scorpions. After that, Mikey was never seen at a Teazers' club again, despite having frequented the clubs for years. One has to ask how Lolly knew that it would be in his interests to distance himself from his friend at a time when no one knew of Mikey's involvement in the Kebble case.

About a month before he died, in early April of 2010, Lolly sent Ricardo an MMS of his bleeding face being attended to in a hospital.

The message came out of the blue and shocked all of us in the office. As we all frantically attempted to get hold of him, Robyn, Ricardo and I thought the apparent assault had either something to do with the Michael Kalymnios case, or perhaps with ex-friend and business partner Mark Andrews (with whom Lolly had an ongoing dispute). But an hour or so later when he arrived at the office, Lolly was all smiles despite a deep hole in the back of his head and on his right cheek. This immediately told us it couldn't have been a beating as, had that been the case, Lolly would have been incensed. It turned out that he had walked into the monkey cage at his house with a little too much aggression and Mikey the monkey – not Schultz! – had decided this was his realm and not Lolly's. Mikey had jumped down and attacked Lolly, biting his cheek and the back of his head.

We all asked what had happened to Mikey. Lolly smiled and acknowledged that it had been his fault, not the monkey's, an unusual admission for Lolly and an understanding only possible in his interactions with animals. Who would have known it would take a capuchin monkey to make Lolly admit he was wrong?

Mere weeks before his death, Lolly's morbid mood suddenly lifted. It appeared that an offer to purchase the Teazers' business was imminent and Adult World's Arthur Calamaras had sent an employee from Cape Town to undertake a due diligence process of the group. Lolly had made peace with his decision: he would sell it all and move on with his life. While Ricardo confirmed that an offer to purchase was on the cards, he also assured me that Lolly would take care of Ricardo, Robyn and myself, and that this could be the start of exciting new endeavours for us all. This possibility vastly improved Lolly's mood, and to add to this he was extremely excited when he forwarded the following email to me about a week before he was killed:

Dear Mr Jackson

I would like to invite you to address the 'XYZ' Gentlemen's Dinner group at a private dinner evening on the 12th May 2010.

The event is a meeting of our dinner and discussion group, 'XYZ'. The group was formed in 1987 with the aim of learning about a variety of subjects, especially topical and controversial issues.

Private, formal, black tie dinner meetings are held every 2nd Wednesday of the month at the 'ABC' dining room, at which a guest speaker is invited to give a 20 to 40 minute talk, after which the members ask questions and raise relevant points.

There are 22 male-only members who are in the 40 to 65 age group. We represent a cross-section of professional activity, including engineering, quantity surveying, automotive retail, medicine, computing, manufacturing, lawyers, shipping, publishing and life insurance.

Although members may invite guests, attendance at each meeting is limited to approximately 40.

Topics have often been of a political nature, with several speakers from a broad range of political viewpoints including speakers such as the ANC (Azhar Cachalia and

Penuell Maduna), the Conservative Party (Beyers de Klerk) and the AWB (Eugene Terre'Blanche) amongst others. Dr Zac de Beer has also honoured us with an interesting presentation.

But there have also been speakers on non-political topics [and these] have included Hansie Cronje, Jules Browde SC, Govan Reddy, John Gordon Davis, Bruce Fordyce, Bill Schreiner, Peter Vundla, Mistress Di, Warren Clewlow and others.

As a colourful and controversial figure, I thought it would be interesting for our members to hear from you of your experiences in setting a very successful business under very difficult conditions. Also '**Lolly Jackson, The Man**' from what I read on your website, is I know of interest to our members.

I look forward to receive [sic] your reply as to your willingness and availability on the 12th May.

Regards,

Keith.

It was the kind of recognition that he craved and a proud Lolly confirmed his attendance. With much-renewed vigour I was instructed to put together a presentation as well as a speech for the occasion.

Five days later, Lolly was dead.

7

THE AFTERMATH

Tuesday, 4 May 2010

It was 4.00 am and although I was exhausted, I couldn't sleep. Every time I closed my eyes, I saw the vivid blood smear on the wall at the murder scene. I eventually gave up and decided to wade through the mass of emails that had already come flooding in. An hour later, I received my first phone call from the media. It was Rahima Essop of *Eyewitness News*. She wanted an interview outside Lolly's Bedfordview house, evidently unaware that for the past few months Lolly hadn't called it home as he was living in Kyalami.

Demi had, as a result of her marital problems, been staying with her mother at 40 Kloof Road, but in order to protect the marriage I couldn't allow the media to find her there and ask questions about why her husband was living in Kyalami. I convinced Rahima that everyone would be meeting at Teazers Rivonia.

At 6.00 am, on my way to our Rivonia office, I walked into a Shell garage on Marlboro Drive and was jarred by a familiar sound coming from the radio – it was my voice, crying on the phone to Demi while informing her that her husband had been murdered, the sound clip courtesy of Mandy Wiener's earlier recording. Adding to my horror was a newspaper headline screaming: *Lolly Gunned Down*. I grabbed a copy of the newspaper and ran out of the shop – tears already blurring my vision. I recall thinking quietly, 'Boss, you finally made every front page.'

My phone had been wailing ever since Rahima had broken the ice. I needed a breather and Ricardo and I set up an early breakfast at the News Café in Rivonia. We were to be joined later at the Rivonia club by Shaun Russouw, Lolly's partner from the Durban club, after he'd driven up to Johannesburg. When he joined us, Shaun looked haggard, but was clearly ready for anything – he handed me an LM5 assault rifle to hold while he gathered his things from the car.

Once inside the office, we hung about aimlessly waiting for Lolly's family to join us. We three seemed to share the same unspoken emotions: shock, grief and a disconcerting feeling of disorientation. I wondered what would happen to Teazers and to all of us. I shied away from addressing any press-related matters as I wasn't sure this was still my designated role. Shortly after 9.30 am, Demi, Samantha and Manoli arrived, with Lolly's long-time business partner Paul De Jager in tow (Paul would, in a matter of days, be granted full control of the Teazers' group by Demi). The family, along with Paul, went into Lolly's office to decide the business's fate. The first decision was to close all Teazers' branches for the day. Although Lolly would probably have wanted his business to keep running, realistically this was not an option.

Ricardo was called in and, a short while later, it was my turn. Demi said that as Lolly had trusted me to handle the press, I'd be the spokesperson for the Teazers' group as well as the Jackson family. This meant I had to get back on point, and immediately went down the stairs to face a throng of media people who had converged outside. What followed was the most exhausting day of my life. Trying to cobble the Lolly Jackson murder saga into usable stories for the various media platforms was physically and emotionally draining.

While still outside, I had noticed that a locksmith had entered the building. When I had finished briefing the press, I went upstairs to find that the office safes had been opened and boxes were quickly being filled with cash. In addition to the money being shifted, bundles of documents were also being removed. It seems that Lolly's alleged latest will had apparently been taken from the safe behind the wood-panelled shelving in his private lounge bar. Robyn Teixeira told me that the 2005 version of the will was not the most recent. 'I signed witness to a will and it was probably two months before [Lolly died] with Alan [Allschwang]. As I was initialling, I glanced over the content and I know that mentioned in there was his [Lolly's] partner from Durban, his partner from Cape Town, the youngest son Julian and the SPCA.' (*scan QR code 6 on page 218 to listen to this interview*)

According to the 2005 will, the executors of Lolly's estate were Demi, Samantha and Manoli (the latter at age 21), with Demi bizarrely being granted right of veto. Also peculiar was the fact that no mention was made here of

Ricardo, Greg Fedele (from the Cape Town club) or Shaun Russouw being nominated as beneficiaries, which was not in accordance with the document Robyn says she signed. None of this seemed to fit, especially when I remembered what Lolly's ex-wife Sharon had to say about his first heart attack.

I left the pillaged room to take a walk and clear my head, and found Robyn and Ricardo in the dark passage at the back end of the main floor that led to the dancers' change rooms. Even in the muddied light, Ricardo's pain was visible. I put my arm around him and he began to heave in anguish. None of us were related, but our mutual loyalty to Lolly bound us together as surely as if we were family. Somehow, we had to get through this.

After recovering his composure, Ricardo verified that Paul and Demi were moving the money and documents to Lolly's Kyalami house. He mentioned that we were supposed to make sure Demi's belongings found their way back there too. This, we both understood, would be undertaken under the cover of darkness. We had to persuade onlookers that Demi and Lolly were living together at the time of his murder. We couldn't do otherwise – Demi was the boss now.

Later, Ricardo was given the unenviable task – along with Lolly's brother Costa (real name: Constantine) – of identifying Lolly's body. Ricardo had Lolly's fake Cypriot passport (secured by George Smith) and, in the absence of Lolly's ID document, he now had to use this for identification purposes.

Just as the day started feeling more normal, Greg Fedele arrived from Cape Town. The look on his face left no room for error – the man meant business. He said he'd heard that Demi and the children thought they were now in charge. 'This is fucking bullshit!' he shouted (mercifully, Demi had already left). He added that he and Shaun were the only living directors of the company and that if it was a fight Demi wanted, she would have it. He continued ranting, telling us that not a single item was to leave the premises. Later Shaun would agree that it wasn't common practice for a business to automatically be taken over by family members when there were business partners involved. On Greg's instruction, we then gathered in the bar area. He poured us each a substantial drink, which we raised in honour of Lolly. Standing there in the half-light, I sensed this would be the last time we would all get together as one. A terrible schism was about to occur, and our group was to be ripped apart.

Early that evening, while Shaun and Greg rifled through the office filing system for a copy of the 'missing' will, Paul De Jager arrived with a friend from the Germiston SAPS, Colonel Steyn. Steyn then escorted Robyn, Ricardo and myself to Lolly's private lounge to show us a photograph of a man we'd soon find out was George Smith.

He asked if we knew the man and when we had last seen him. It seemed George was the police's prime suspect. At this point Shaun entered the office and handed me a copy of the affidavit that George had deposed and signed with Ian Jordaan – while Lolly was in prison – over the Michael Kalymnios case. The timing was impeccable as Ricardo and I had, only the night before, mentioned the affidavit and now Shaun had managed to find it! Colonel Steyn quickly seized the document and left.

Wednesday, 5 May 2010

I'd just settled at my desk, when I heard a commotion downstairs. The *Carte Blanche* team had arrived and I'd completely forgotten that they had an appointment. After scrambling to help them set up for the interview, I had a few seconds to compose myself before the cameras started rolling and Devi Sankaree Govender began to give me the third degree.

The focus of the interview was Johannesburg's seedy underbelly – its crime, money laundering and corruption, as well as Lolly's involvement in it – rather than his murder. My impression was that this story had been prepared months in advance with the expectation that it could be made into a show at a moment's notice (as no doubt Lolly would be arrested for money laundering or a similar charge at some stage). His death evidently proved too good an opportunity to miss.

Just before the interview began, Devi told me that Lolly's Jeep had been found in Kings Road, Bedfordview the night before. My mind racing, I answered her questions as best I could, while not betraying what was actually taking place in my head. We would have been fools not to know who players like Radovan Krejcir were, especially after Ricardo had told us to Google him to see what crimes he stood accused of in his native Czech Republic. Lolly had asked us to keep a constant eye on the rand–dollar exchange rate, which, if favourable, inevitably resulted a few days later in cash being loaded into Globe Flight courier bags that were hastily collected by non-courier-company employees.

As I'd never received a definite explanation from Lolly himself as to the nature of these transactions, I was certainly not going to blacken his name based on my suspicions. Ricardo was more schooled in the actual goings-on of the business, while Lolly and I had an agreement – the less I knew, the easier it would be for me to deny any knowledge of dubious business practices at a later stage.

With the interview over, I once more felt the crushing exhaustion I'd experienced the day before. I wasn't the only one feeling this way – both Ricardo and Robyn wore the same fatigued expressions on their faces. Unbeknown to me, while I was being raked over the coals by *Carte Blanche*, all hell was breaking loose in Lolly's office. Ian Jordaan had arrived with Demi and the family, and they were now locked in a heated dispute with Greg and Shaun over who was running the show. The battle lines had been drawn. Shaun eventually left and reminded us all that, since everything we'd seen and heard was privileged information, there would be dire consequences if anything was leaked.

On my way downstairs to assemble the staff for a meeting, I was told by Greg to grab the first photographer I could find as it was imperative we release a message of unity to the public and press. Chris Collingridge, chief lens man for *The Star*, quickly took some shots of Demi, Manoli and Samantha. I saw that Chris was absorbing every word and gesture so after I felt he'd heard enough, I tapped him on the shoulder and asked for privacy.

Demi, in an attempt to further this appearance of solidarity, had announced to the staff that Robyn would still be doing administrative work from home. She even went into detail, outlining the laptop and 3G card Robyn needed to do the job. The truth was that Robyn had resigned two weeks prior to Lolly's death (Lolly had asked her to keep quiet about the resignation), but Demi evidently didn't want to take the chance that this resignation could be seen as defection as it would weaken the already diminishing morale at Teazers.

Watching from the sidelines with Ricardo, I was struck by how quickly the enthusiasm Lolly had engendered in his staff had been replaced with feelings of dread and concern. After the meeting, and once her family had left, I approached Demi and asked if we could go to a coffee shop for a quiet word.

Once settled, I asked her if she knew that Lolly had agreed to be my daughter Alexis's godfather, which she confirmed.

My next question was: what would happen to the house my family and I were living in? 'Lolly would have wanted you to have the house and he would have wanted you to be there for me,' she answered. 'Play the game and give me the loyalty you gave Lolly. As long as there's a Jackson alive, you and your family will never have to worry about the roof over your heads. It's what he would have wanted, Sean, and I'll make it happen.' After this reassurance, Demi told me to make sure any rumours of a divorce were immediately dispelled.

As things stood at that moment, I had a choice – play the game or face the prospect of becoming homeless. In the days that followed, I fulfilled my role to the best of my abilities. I'm not proud of what I did, but it was what needed to be done to protect my wife and three-month-old daughter.

The rest of the day was spent fielding more interviews and briefing the press about protocol on 'opening night' – when we re-opened the clubs after Lolly's death.

Thursday, 6 May 2010

Three days after Lolly's death, I made my way to the Johannesburg Magistrates Court as it was the day that had been set aside for Lolly to have appeared regarding the Michael Kalymnios case. I met with Joanne Rizotto, a lawyer from Ian Jordaan's firm who also happened to be Ian's girlfriend, to try to get the case dismissed as well as to retrieve the bail money. Back in February, Lolly's legal team (consisting of Ian, Barry Roux and Kenny Oldwadge) had found it highly amusing that I was badgered into signing for Lolly's bail as they hated standing in queues, which left me as the only viable candidate. Ian joked, 'Chin up, *boet*. We just gave you job security', knowing that Lolly couldn't get rid of me without losing his R5 000. After Joanne had spoken to the magistrate, she told us that the death certificate would have to be presented before the charges could be dismissed. Eventually, the magistrate heard our case and it was dismissed.

Friday, 7 May 2010

By now the Lolly Jackson murder saga had begun to retreat from the headlines, but a barrage of condolences started flooding in. They were all raw and heartfelt, and sent from a cross-section of the community. Literally hundreds of people expressed deep loss and sadness – people whose lives Lolly had once touched. After the emotionally draining past few days, these letters somehow afforded me a measure of comfort. No matter what the public perception was, and despite the fact that Lolly was something of a rogue, he was apparently appreciated at least as much as he was hated.

That afternoon, I released details of the funeral to the public: there was to be a private ceremony followed by a public burial. Next, I had our printer create an oversized portrait of Lolly that would take centre stage at the burial. It was his favourite and had graced the cover of his 2006 biography. In it, he was dressed in a tuxedo and he would always refer to it as 'The Don' photo.

Sunday, 9 May 2010

My task for the day was to fetch the newly framed portrait and take it to show Demi. She asked if I could leave it there overnight and collect it the next morning. That evening, I watched the *Carte Blanche* episode I'd been interviewed for earlier in the week.

As I watched, an old enemy of Lolly's made an appearance: Andrew Phillips – owner of strip club The Grand. He was followed by an ex-Teazers dancer who had worked for Lolly before 'defecting'. I was deeply offended by what she said about the alleged human trafficking at Teazers, which as far as

I could make out was totally fabricated. A few weeks earlier I'd witnessed Lolly's rage over the way in which she'd left Teazers.

There had always been rumours and controversy surrounding the way in which Lolly brought the dancers into South Africa. In the early years, he would try to lubricate the process by giving Eastern European embassy workers Louis Vuitton bags and gifts, while visiting their respective countries. When this was seen as bribery, he used a standard method which was adopted not only by Teazers but other businesses within the adult entertainment industry.

Prior to my joining Teazers, there had been several brushes with the law regarding alleged human trafficking and the retaining of dancers' passports. As a result, company procedure pertaining to the 'importing' of strippers followed a new regimen.

Firstly, an overseas agent would send Teazers a photograph of the dancer seeking employment (or the girl would do so herself). Where agents were involved, the stripper would enter into a separate contract with them (just as Teazers did with the agent). The girls were then sent a breakdown of what their potential earnings and expenses might be. Teazers would then send the dancer an invitation which she'd take to her embassy and apply for a visa (*see Appendix 5 on page 231*).

On confirmation, Teazers would book an open-ended ticket for the dancer (costs to be subtracted from her wages). In terms of an agreement between Teazers and Home Affairs, if a dancer wanted to leave Teazers, she'd have to exit the country and then re-enter (any admin costs being again deducted from her account).

Teazers adopted the relatively pain-free route of using corporate visas in order to save time. When we'd applied as a company and had been rejected, it was decided to use separate companies owned by Shaun and Greg. Now, once the dancer landed on South African soil, Relocation Online (a company specialising in immigration and visa matters) would facilitate the documentation and submit this, along with her passport, to Home Affairs. As long as either Shaun or Greg had signed it, the girl would be granted a work permit. If a dancer wanted to leave in order to work at another strip club, she'd have to be taken off the corporate listing and the certificate had to be made available to Teazers again. I remember how three girls began working for Teazers through a new agent (and former dancer), Oksana. They weren't happy with Lolly's rules, especially the fact that they couldn't have boyfriends or see clients outside of work. Just prior to us deporting them, they left in the middle of the night from the Collins Road house (Bedfordview) with Oksana. When Lolly heard about this, he was furious and demanded that Ricardo get them back to their country of origin. Ricardo couldn't do so and the three 'defected' to The Grand. It was one of these girls who was interviewed on *Carte Blanche* (and bear in mind, she'd only worked at Teazers for a few weeks).

After Lolly's death, the Department of Home Affairs found their passports at one of their Durban branches. They were curious as to why a company based in Durban was issuing corporate certificates to a non-related company. We told them that Teazers had a bilateral trading agreement with the Durban-based company, but they didn't accept this. The entire affair exploded and brought down a rain of nationwide raids, which resulted in a year-long attempt to clear backlogs and court cases so that Teazers could hold onto their dancers. *(scan QR code 7 on page 219 to access a* Noseweek *article on this topic)*

Monday, 10 May 2010

On the day that Lolly Jackson was buried, Lacksom and I collected the photographic portrait of Lolly from Demi and headed over to Teazers Rivonia to meet up with the other staff members who'd be attending the service. My only memory of the funeral is of Robyn clutching my hand desperately and sobbing the whole way through. The Greek priest overseeing the burial was the same gentleman who'd come to our offices in January to bless the clubs.

Once we got to the gravesite, I urged the media to allow the family and mourners access to enough space so they could feel comfortable. The event was brief but I vividly recall Vince Marino, Lolly's oldest friend and biographer, delivering a heart-wrenching eulogy. He offered me the chance to speak, but feeling too emotional, I declined.

After Vince's speech we lined up to drop earth onto Lolly's coffin, which had been draped in a Greek flag I'd bought the previous Saturday. While mourners were standing near the picture, a sudden gust of wind tore it down from the easel and glass shattered everywhere as it hit the ground.

After the service, I caught up with Lolly's youngest son, Julian. He was a pupil at my old *alma mater*, St Andrew's, in Bloemfontein. Julian had not been allowed to travel to the venue in the family car, but Demi's sister and her husband had. Robyn and I were sickened by this when we talked about it later.

Mandy Wiener from *Eyewitness News* approached me as I was leaving and asked if she could convey her sincere condolences to Demi. She showed me her hands, reminiscent of the gesture of a card dealer at a casino, so I could see that she didn't have a recording device with her. I accepted her gesture with a certain wry respect.

8
THE PLOT THICKENS

In the weeks after Lolly's untimely death, the still visibly shaken Demi appeared more regularly at the office. She'd begun to rely heavily on Ricardo and myself to help her get her affairs in order. Demi's fragile emotional state vacillated between deep depression and moments of lucidity when she appeared completely normal, making the occasional joke and enjoying our company.

Robyn was preparing to leave the company, an emotional move for her, and Demi wasn't making it easy. Demi had accused Robyn of selling confidential information to Andrew Phillips for years, a claim she later retracted.

It was clear that Demi and Paul wanted to weed out all those staff members who'd been loyal to Lolly so that Demi could surround herself with those she could manipulate, but they were determined to humiliate Robyn as well. On her last day at Teazers, Paul made Robyn wait for hours before handing over her last salary cheque. Demi ignored her departure, and gave her a dismissive look rather than a goodbye or thank you for her loyalty and years of service.

Demi's staff purge instilled a sense of despair in both Ricardo and myself. We'd both been loyal to Lolly and were both desperate to keep our jobs. Demi explained the change saying that Lolly had been her backbone, but now it was time to grow her own. This apparent shift from saint to sinner didn't ring true; it seemed to us as if Paul and Alan Allschwang (the estate's tax attorney) were ultimately in control. Demi still needed a strong male figure, if not two in this instance, to lead her, but whom she tried to control by playing the victim.

My relationship with Demi changed radically after she allegedly caught Ricardo stealing. While Lolly was still alive Ricardo had been accused by various sources – including Radovan – of having embezzled money belonging to Lolly. Lolly refused to even consider such a thing. Shortly before Lolly was murdered, Radovan again brought up the topic at a lunch with Lolly and Demi, questioning how Ricardo, who had recently bought a new restaurant, could afford to do so on his salary. Lolly again dismissed the matter.

If Ricardo was in fact taking large sums of money from the business, why would Lolly ignore it? There were a number of possible scenarios that could explain it: perhaps there was a standing arrangement between the two designed to compensate Ricardo for his involvement in risky illegal dealings, or perhaps Ricardo knew too much about the illegal matters Lolly was involved in and was being paid to keep quiet. The other possible reason was that, as Ricardo claims, he was depositing large sums of money into his own account and then handing it back to Lolly (after a service fee) in order to hide money from SARS. The situation becomes more complex if we consider that apparently Ricardo was mentioned in Lolly's alleged missing will, and left a ten per cent share of the Teazers' group.

After Lolly's death, Ricardo did everything that Demi and Paul asked of him (and then some), but things were changing and he must have known that the walls were closing in, even going so far as to say that he might soon need a job.

On 21 May 2010, less than three weeks after Lolly had been murdered, I received a panicked phone call from Demi. In her hands she had a copy of a cheque which indisputably showed that Ricardo had changed the Receiver of Revenue's name from 'SARS' to 'R**S** F**AB**RE (**S**alary)' (*see Appendix 6 on page 232*). He'd apparently added his own details in, post signature, as shown by the letters in bold. The 'official' version of what transpired, detailed in affidavits lodged by Ian Jordaan, was that Demi had been alerted by a radio announcement saying that cheques should in future be made out, not to SARS, but to The South African Revenue Service. But the truth is rather different.

The Rivonia branch of Standard Bank, across the road from Teazers, had been robbed so often that it was closed. Ricardo now had to dispatch Lacksom to bank the cheques made out to customers of Standard Bank, as he (Ricardo) could no longer walk across the road and do this himself. On the 4th of May, the day after Lolly's murder, Lacksom had been on his way to the bank when Ricardo called him urgently, saying he needed to bring the cheques back. For some strange reason, Lacksom looked to see who the cheques were made out to.

Six days later, while delivering the portrait of Lolly to

the church for the funeral, Lacksom got caught up in a traffic jam. Idly waiting, he read through the funeral order of service programme and was startled to recognise a name from the previous week's cheques: 'Ricardo Fabre – right hand and friend', read the programme. Lacksom's suspicions were aroused for two reasons. Firstly, he hadn't been aware of Ricardo's surname, but clearly the first name rang a bell. Secondly, Lacksom also knew that the staff were only ever paid on a very specific day of the month. He approached Demi a day or two later and confided his suspicions to her.

Initially, Demi refused to believe that such a thing could be true, but the following Friday with proof in hand, furnished by the astute handyman, she sought Alan Allschwang's counsel. His instructions were to do nothing; stopping payment on the cheques might lead to subsequent difficulties in proving the case. I was asked by Demi to do some investigating of my own, which ironically led to Ricardo confessing to her that he suspected I was spying for someone.

Demi asked if I could gain access to Ricardo's work computer. I was to look out for anything incriminating, back it up, and pass on any information I had found. As a reward, I was again promised that the house my family and I were staying in would be mine.

Back at the office, I locked the doors and got down to work. Ricardo is an avid Batman fan, and on my first guess, typing BATMAN as password, I was in! Slightly disappointed at how easy it was to gain access to Ricardo's files, I downloaded what I needed and headed home with all the data. Over the course of that weekend, Demi and I were in constant contact, preparing evidence to present to Paul De Jager. Alan, in the meantime, was assessing how best to use this information to our advantage with the tax authorities.

On the Monday, Demi and I met privately. She asked

me to plot all the evidence outlining possible payments to Ricardo on a spreadsheet. Instructed to work from her home, I arrived the next day to find boxes of old cheque book stubs and quickly got to work. Once we had this information, it was easy for me to request copies of cheques from the bank, all material that Alan required to draw up a founding affidavit. Many of the cheques that had been returned were missing, either because Ricardo needed to hide the evidence or because Lolly didn't want to have such information floating around. This wasn't unusual, even the GAAP system (point-of-sale software) was cleared every night after cash-ups. Once monies had been tallied, stocks taken and dancer recons expedited, the entire paper trail was routinely shredded.

Within two weeks, and on the Friday before Ricardo was arrested, I went through to Alan's office to sign the affidavit forming the basis for the charges to be laid. While reading through the paperwork, I noticed that it stated that Demi had made the discovery herself. I questioned this and was told by Alan that we should stick to this story in order to protect Lacksom. The affidavit was duly signed and, along with copies of the cheques from the banks and those I'd managed to find myself, a charge of fraud was laid against Ricardo Fabre. The amount was based on the cheque stubs – the assumption being that none of the payments from the past few years had reached SARS – and tallied up to an astonishing R23 million.

Because we had to pull copies of cheques from the bank, there was a substantial cost involved and Alan decided we would have enough once there was conclusive proof of fraud over the R1 million mark (he said any amount over R500 000 carried with it a mandatory sentence of 15 years). The logic was that if we could show alleged theft over a consistent period, then we could estimate to what extent it went.

After leaving Alan and going to the office, I found Paul De Jager, Demi and an auditor holed up in Lolly's private lounge. To say that Paul was angry would be an understatement. He'd discovered that a company in which he held fifty per cent ownership – Tronic Entertainment (the holding company for the Midrand property) – had been seriously defrauded. Paul's nest egg was gone. Secretly, I found this amusing because it was the system Paul had allowed to be put in place that made the fraud possible. In the past Lolly would send cheques through to Paul to sign, after which he'd send them back to Lolly for counter-signing. Paul, frustrated by this apparent waste of time had simply signed multiple blank cheques which were held at the offices for occasions when they were needed. Lolly wielded enormous control over the finances and it seemed Paul had never so much as seen a bank statement over the years they'd been business partners. Even I was canny enough to insist that Lolly and I share a joint bank account when we were about to open up a massage venue at the Rivonia branch!

The auditor then uncovered another unsettling fact: Ricardo had also allegedly been inserting extra figures on the original cheques. So for example, a cheque made out for R4 000, was transformed into one for R44 000. This set the powder keg alight and Alan was given the order to proceed with legal action immediately.

As we were about to leave the office, I fell into a heated argument with Paul who had refused to hand over our salary cheques. He pulled me aside and explained that he had no issue paying me, but there was no chance he would give 'that thieving bastard' his. A flaw in this plan was that when I cashed my salary cheque, the bank would call Ricardo to notify him. Lolly hated the constant payday salary clearance calls, and had ironically changed the contact number on the account to none other than the man now accused of plundering the accounts.

When Lolly fired an employee or dancer, they resigned or else went back overseas, he was happy to hand pay cheques over to them as he knew full well that these payments could easily be stopped, and often were. Ricardo was constantly inundated with calls from dancers whose cheques had been cancelled.

My unease was growing, and to add to it, I received a call later that night from Colonel van Heerden, the investigating officer in Lolly's murder case. He wanted to know why there was a copy of an affidavit, deposed by me, sitting on his desk on a Friday night. I explained that while our lawyers had handled the entire affair, I was the only person with the authority to lay charges as no executors had been appointed at this stage. In other words, I was the fool who'd be shouldering the consequences of yet another messy situation. Van Heerden understood and told me he'd be the one to arrest Ricardo on 31 May 2010 at Teazers Rivonia.

The day I was dreading finally arrived and, as usual, Ricardo and I met for coffee before work at News Café Rivonia. Looking tired and drawn, I was tempted to tell him to make a run for it, but instead stifled the impulse. The auditor's presence in the office must have alerted Ricardo to trouble brewing and he warned me that if something went wrong, both of our standing deals would be disregarded so that others could get more money for themselves. He added that he and I were 'fucked' and that our loyalty to Lolly would be the death of us.

I was distressed, watching him wrestle with his private demons; aware that, in a matter of hours, his life as he knew it would be destroyed. I was left feeling that our special team had now been disbanded and that I'd be on my own when contemplating just how long I'd be seen as useful. Together we walked slowly down the road towards the club for the last time, silence adding to the already morose mood we shared.

As Ricardo went upstairs, I picked up a call from Colonel van Heerden asking where Ricardo was and telling me to stay put. From a vantage point, I watched as they led my friend away. Filled with disgust and self-loathing it was hard to face calls from people like Robyn wanting to know what had happened.

Demi and Paul took great pains to distance themselves from Ricardo's arrest. Neither were present at the Rivonia branch on the day, but both stayed close to their cellphones waiting for updates and constantly calling me. When Ricardo's fiancée Nichol frantically called Demi after the incident, Demi claimed to know nothing about it.

They'd arrested the one man who could unravel the financial mysteries of Teazers, and that's exactly what Ricardo did – to SARS. Alan, through the mouthpiece of Ian, had attempted to have Ricardo's bail denied, but Ricardo succeeded in being released on his forty-second birthday, for the sum of R10 000. I found it amusing that, at his bail application hearing, Ricardo let slip some details about Lolly's pending divorce as well as the alleged missing will. (*scan QR code 8 on page 219 to read IOL article 'Mystery Surrounds Lolly's Missing Will'*)

Demi hadn't anticipated Ricardo's airing these allegations, and would soon come to regret the collateral damage of her decision to prosecute. After numerous postponements, a trial date was eventually set and an end was in sight. However, Ricardo's attorneys were forced to withdraw due to a conflict of interest pertaining to a state witness, forcing a further delay to March 2012.

The Ricardo Fabre case is just part of the seedy, greedy infighting that has defined the Teazers' group since Lolly's demise. Unfortunately, customers had begun to avoid the clubs after news of Lolly's death hit the headlines, as these reports exposed the life he apparently led behind the scenes. The danger and mystery surrounding the incident served only to intensify their fear of being caught at one of our clubs, and profits subsequently went down. A welcome respite came in the form of the Soccer World Cup on Sunday 27 June 2010, the game between Argentina and Mexico. The club was quiet until after the game and the last customer left at 6.00 am the next morning. We notched up record takings for the night, triggering a boom period.

But profit margins fell even though we were advertising more than ever. Paul installed expensive smoking areas in both the Midrand and Rivonia branches, later enclosed with curtains in the Rivonia club to increase the small Teaze-Hers capacity. The changes within the venue were not only cosmetic. Originally, Lolly had the staff structured in the form of a pyramid, with a strong apex, but this had become inverted and senior management had become top-heavy.

While Paul and Demi seemed to be calling the shots, Shaun Russouw from Teazers Durban instituted a multi-million rand claim against the group in November 2011 for unpaid fees for the use of his corporate permits, which were used to bring in foreign dancers. Teazers was now facing the possible loss of a substantial amount of money, and in an effort to deal with the claim, the Teazers' lawyers entered into negotiations with Ricardo. In exchange for dropping charges against him, they requested he sign affidavits relating to the Russouw case. These documents disputed the amount Russouw was claiming – stating there was no clear formula used to determine the amount – and also added that the Teazers' group had used their own agents for procuring dancers. Ricardo Fabre signed the affidavits on 7 December 2011.

The affidavit begs the question: why would Teazers drop the Fabre case to gain a two-paragraph document that doesn't hold any explosive information? Was it to remove the possibility that Ricardo might expose more than they'd bargained for? Whatever the reason, Ricardo has effectively been halted from detailing those matters he'd threatened to reveal in court, matters the Teazers' management and their legal team would rather let rest.

More theories came to light in August 2010. Demi told me that Robyn and Ricardo's cellphone records for the period surrounding Lolly's murder had been pulled, and the results told a worrying story. Apparently, Robyn and Ricardo had been chatting up a storm to Radovan with as many as 20 calls a day. Various interpretations included the story of how Robyn and Ricardo were involved in a money-laundering scheme. It would have been easy to facilitate, as both Robyn and Ricardo had access to the dancers' personal accounts. By dint of the sheer number of accounts they allegedly handled, the Reserve Bank limits wouldn't have taken note of the transactions, and it was speculated that a possible motive could be the measly salaries they drew. The speculation escalated to new heights when it was suggested the he, Lolly, had threatened to expose Robyn and Ricardo when he went public with Alekos Panayi, the bank manager at Laiki Bank who had facilitated a money-laundering scheme.

This was when Lolly's most trusted staff members, according to speculation, became accomplices to his murder. The cellphone records allegedly show that on the Monday Lolly died Robyn went to a coffee shop in Craighall Park – far from her home in the south of Johannesburg. She was, according to theory, waiting for a call from Ricardo to confirm that Lolly had been killed. Cellphone records allegedly support the idea that Robyn had then called Radovan to confirm the death and the three would then prepare to put on an act of grief and sorrow. However, as I saw Robyn and Ricardo immediately after they'd heard of Lolly's murder, such acting would have been a tough ask of Al Pacino; in my mind it was impossible that they had anything to do with the crime.

This atmosphere of suspicion and speculation gripped everyone, but very often went nowhere. These stories simply faded into obscurity.

At this time Demi started claiming that those responsible for Lolly's murder were now also targeting her. She wanted to buy a new car as her current one, a Mercedes SL, was too conspicuous. I was told to buy a Mazda 3 MPS to act as a decoy to her Mercedes. Without ever seeing the car, she signed the papers and, the very next day, gave me over R300 000 in cash which I took to the dealership. I then had to arrange insurance and armour-plated windows for the Mazda. During this time, Demi began mentioning her long-lost cousin, Tyrel Manson, and I was instructed to register the car in his name. To this day, I've never seen her drive this car.

9

THE FANTASY UNRAVELS

On 25 September 2010, I received an hysterical call from Demi. Paul O'Sullivan, alleged former British MI5 agent, former head of ACSA (Airports Company South Africa) security and the man who would ultimately be responsible for taking down Police Commissioner Jackie Selebi, wanted a meeting with her, saying that SARS was after her. He wanted Demi to provide information on Radovan as it seemed he thought she'd been privy to the money laundering that had taken place between her husband and the Czech. If she failed to do so, he intimated she'd lose control of the entire Teazers' group. She told me that O'Sullivan had offered to cut a deal for her with SARS that would see her left with the ownership of two clubs. Alan would later rubbish this, saying it was nonsense and the 'offer' should be ignored. Demi seemed unwilling to meet with O'Sullivan and we arranged that I would go in her place. This was not my first contact with O'Sullivan, and certainly wouldn't be my last.

I had been fascinated with O'Sullivan, who appeared to be one of the rare good guys. He seemed to be a crusader of justice, looking to rid the streets of criminals. Not one to shy away from making enemies, O'Sullivan stirred up trouble while employed as head of security for ACSA. He was displeased with the level of service provided by a security sub-contractor with the result that this contract – a deal worth an alleged R130 million per year – was terminated. But in his digging, he'd ruffled the feathers of then Police Commissioner Jackie Selebi and O'Sullivan was summarily dismissed.

This sparked a war against other corrupt operations Jackie had been involved in and O'Sullivan soon uncovered a relationship between Jackie and notoriously crooked businessman Glenn Agliotti. I was full of respect for O'Sullivan, a man who, with little concern for his own safety, was intent on bringing down his powerful foes.

As a result of the highly publicised Selebi case, O'Sullivan gained much respect and credibility. I held the same opinion and believed him to be a fearless, determined crusader of the law. I was pleased to hear from Mandy Wiener that O'Sullivan was involved in investigating Lolly's case.

I made contact with O'Sullivan and he insisted that we meet at a public venue – the Sandton City Shopping Centre – at 6.00 pm. In true James Bond style, I was to receive SMS instructions once I arrived there. My next destination was the foyer of the Michelangelo Hotel. This evidently wasn't meant to be the final meeting place, but I identified O'Sullivan ascending the escalator and approached him. He appeared flustered at having been discovered unprepared, but asked me to follow him – which in itself became quite an adventure. He led me through the fire-escape stairwell, then through gates that looked as if they should have been locked, until we eventually reached a landing after having climbed numerous flights of stairs. O'Sullivan paused momentarily to listen for anything untoward then we proceeded to the Business Centre in Sandton Square. Having convinced himself that we weren't being followed, O'Sullivan made himself a cup of tea and we settled down on the balcony overlooking the interior of the mall – Paul positioning himself so as to be able to carefully view his surroundings.

We began discussing Lolly and I expressed my concerns that the case was seemingly making little progress. O'Sullivan bluntly told me that as far as he was concerned senior members of the police would see to it that the case drifted into obscurity.

During the conversation I felt that O'Sullivan was carefully evaluating me, searching for weaknesses he could exploit. Looking back, it feels as though he used my loyalty towards Lolly and my desire to see justice served to encourage me to disclose information. O'Sullivan kept making reference to Radovan, insisting the Czech would be arrested and deported by the end of August 2010, and that there were numerous people in his native land who wished to see the man dead. (*scan QR code 9 on page 219 to read IOL article 'Czech Linked to Lolly Killing Here to Stay'*)

Next, he brought up Uwe Gemballa – the German sportscar conversion specialist who had been suffocated to death – and inquired if Gemballa had, in fact, spent two nights at Lolly's house before his fateful disappearance. I was shocked; prior to Lolly's murder, I'd never even heard the name, and now the German's death was being linked to Lolly! Seeming to accept that I didn't know anything, O'Sullivan shifted to the topic of money laundering, again placing emphasis on Radovan's involvement. I said that it appeared that Lolly had been part of some illegal dealings but that I wasn't at liberty to give voice to my assumptions. The only person who could answer this question conclusively was Ricardo Fabre.

O'Sullivan then really rattled me. He stated he'd been approached by Alekos Panayi after a fight with Lolly, and had helped Alekos depose the money-laundering affidavits with the intention of bringing Lolly to justice. But what was probably the most shocking, was when he told me how he was being fed information from inside Teazers and had compiled a 90-page dossier on all of Lolly's illicit dealings. I asked if I could view the dossier, but O'Sullivan declined. He did, however, offer his investigative services in respect of the murder case for a hefty down payment of R100 000, payable up front. In return, he assured me he would keep Demi and me well informed of developments in the case.

Totally thrown by what had transpired, I declined his offer. Our meeting drew to a close with Paul requesting a detailed statement from me outlining everything I knew. This I was not willing to do as I assured him I knew very little.

In a later incident in July, I had received a call from O'Sullivan during which he claimed that Radovan wanted me dead. He insisted that only he could ensure my survival, but the price would be my complete cooperation, including making a statement regarding everything I knew. I was frightened and totally thrown by the call. I confided in both Demi and Alan who felt this was yet another attempt to extract information. Should O'Sullivan contact me, I was to make it known that under no circumstances would I be giving any statements and he should refrain from contacting me again.

O'Sullivan duly called me the following week, asking why I hadn't been in touch. As I had come to discover, it was customary for him to offer a token of information in an attempt to lubricate our discussion – he told me Ricardo was now a marked man. I explained that I was a witness in Ricardo's case and thus could not discuss it. I was, however, more than willing to give him Ricardo's number. I ended by asking him not to contact me further. As was also customary with him, O'Sullivan's response was simply, 'Right'.

Nevertheless, he called me again a few weeks later and said he was off to Europe on business and offered to make a stop-over in Cyprus where he could exert pressure on George Smith, the prime suspect in Lolly's murder, who'd fled to Cyprus after the killing. The asking price for this 'service' would be R40 000. I broached the topic with Demi who declined due to the cost.

To be honest, O'Sullivan's *modus operandi* unnerved me. With every call and contact he made I became more rattled. His persistence and pure tenacity was terrifying as I felt he was trying to wear me down to be used as a pawn in a much bigger game. Over the years, his methods of operating have earned him the name 'Docket Killer' by the police – Radovan would make use of a far more abrasive term: 'cockroach'. His crusade against the Czech has yet to bring Radovan to book.

At the end of September, with uncertainty and manoeverings all around, I reviewed my position at Teazers and with a heavy heart decided to resign. Fearing I was headed for The Grand, Paul De Jager panicked and offered to increase my salary. Demi secretly offered me an additional monthly cash injection of R5 000, to be paid under the table, as long as Paul was kept in the dark. I hate to admit this, but fear and greed enticed me to accept both offers.

Almost two weeks later, Alan asked Demi to get me to find documents relating to Lolly's beloved and now infamous Pagani Zonda on a backup I'd been instructed to make of Lolly's computer before Paul De Jager began using it. My search was fruitless, so I went through each individual folder. In 'My Received Files', I stumbled upon a Microsoft Messenger file and was horrified by what I saw.

Demi had been engaged in an intimate sex chat with the man she'd described to me as her 'cousin', Tyrel Manson! I was overwhelmed by shock and anger. When I registered the date these messages were sent, I was beside myself – Demi's 'sex chat' conversation happened only four days after Lolly's funeral! My anger was not only towards her but also towards myself. I felt used. I was angry at her for manipulating my loyalty towards Lolly. She'd played on my emotions and I felt that I'd let my family down, believing that Demi would look after us in the same way that Lolly had, and in doing this, I'd compromised the relationship with my family. After discovering page upon page of badly written banter, explicit and detailed, I could no longer lie to myself. I had always felt sorry for her – Lolly's infidelities were hard for her to bear and I'd often tried to comfort and reassure her by telling her that Lolly loved her, but here I was – played like a fool.

The next day, I was scheduled to meet with Demi at a consultation with her psychic, with whom she would frequently consult about the business and Lolly. The psychic was going to 'ask' Lolly what he wanted Demi to do with Teazers. In a flurry I called the spiritual advisor and blurted out what I'd just discovered. Without a moment's hesitation, she admitted to knowing of the relationship and said that Tyrel and Demi were soul mates. It later emerged that Demi had also revealed her relationship with Tyrel to Robyn. (*scan QR code 10 on page 219 to listen to this interview*)

When the three of us met later that afternoon, Demi's psychic said, 'Sean, Lolly says you found something and need to share it with Demi', so I told her what I knew. Instantly, Demi became defensive but then blurted out that she didn't care who knew of her affair. With my newly rejuvenated career prospects seemingly on the chopping block, I mumbled that I was happy for her. In hindsight, I'm sickened by the cowardice I showed, but at least it meant there was one less strand in the web of deceit.

Towards the end of 2010, Demi set up a lunch with Radovan at the News Café in Rivonia. After a short while I got a call from her asking me to join the meeting, with express instruction to bring a notepad and pen.

On arrival I was met with not only her and Radovan, but also Cyril Beeka. Demi requested that I draw up a memorandum of understanding whereby Radovan would take control of Teazers, in lieu of the millions in loans owed to him by Lolly. She would remain a shareholder and get roughly 20 per cent of the profits but it would be Radovan who ran the show. Using Cyril's connections, he would bring foreign girls into the country to bolster the dwindling number of dancers. Radovan would also invest money in the business to bring it back to the same standards it had enjoyed while Lolly was still alive. After a still-to-be-determined period of time, Radovan would decide if he wanted to purchase the business outright, a decision that would be based on performance. Should he decide to do so, then his investment and loans would act as part payment, and the balance would be determined at the time a decision was taken.

A few weeks earlier, I had met Brett Kebble's self-confessed killers when I had been sent by Demi to wish Radovan happy birthday. Demi had missed a lunch with Radovan, and to calm him down she gave me money for a birthday gift and I bought a Mont Blanc pen. Mikey Schultz, Faizel 'Kappie' Smith and Nigel McGurk were sitting with Radovan and Jerome Safi, enjoying a couple of drinks while celebrating the birthday. During the course of conversation I was told that the three men would be operating security for the clubs when Radovan took over.

In due course, it became apparent that the vast amounts of money owed to SARS meant any potential sale or investment would be wasted money should SARS foreclose. This was the last we heard of Radovan taking over Teazers.

Soon afterwards I attended a lunch with Demi, Radovan and Mike Hatton-Jones, the bank manager. By the end of the meal, after a fair amount to drink, Sam, Demi and myself ended up at Demi's house. We met Tyrel and I was delighted to see how gentle and attentive he was with her – it looked as if this relationship was the complete opposite of the one she shared with Lolly.

Unfortunately, despite feeling that the relationship between Demi and myself was slowly improving, I suddenly learnt that the house my family and I were occupying had actually been sold. This bombshell was delivered courtesy of a phone call I got from the estate agent – the new owners wanted to come around for an inspection. I was still reeling from the shock of this when, at a Teazers' Christmas party shortly afterwards, the inebriated girlfriend of a staff member accosted Demi, pointed at me and blurted out, 'He's so far up your [Demi's] arse.' My dignity was shattered, but I stood up, resigned on the spot and stormed out of the venue.

The next day, I met with Paul De Jager and confirmed

that I no longer wanted to work for Teazers. My passion and drive had dried up. I'd stay on until the end of January 2011, but for me there was no turning back.

At the same Christmas party, Demi had ended up telling the staff about her relationship with Tyrel. Early in the New Year, she asked me to draw up a letter of employment for him. He'd be paid a sum of R25 000 per month in return for which he'd handle her day-to-day affairs and take over some of her responsibilities at Teazers such as admin and monitoring of the accounts. I left without saying goodbye to Demi and gave in to my emotions on the way home. I wept for Lolly and for the days that would no longer be. An uncertain future lay before me.

The fantasy was unravelling.

On my final working day at Teazers in mid-February of 2011, Paul O'Sullivan asked me to meet him at the McDonald's on Louis Botha Avenue. When I arrived he asked me, in light of the fact that I now had more time on my hands, if I would be prepared to approach Radovan with a view to working for him. While I would be paid by the Czech, it would be Paul that I really worked for; reporting back Radovan's movements, who he met, and any conversations I may have overheard.

Feeling uncomfortable, I went to see Radovan the next evening and told him everything Paul and I had spoken about. He advised that I decline the offer, which I did. I felt that I had been placed in the unenviable position of playing informant, something I would not do.

To the delight of the press in March 2011, O'Sullivan became embroiled in an email-based altercation with

Radovan's attorneys. He stated that they were accepting blood money by representing a fugitive (*see Appendix 7 on page 233*).

Krejcir's attorneys would later take the matter to court, with the result being that O'Sullivan had to apologise to his adversary's attorneys. (*scan QR code 11 on page 219 to access* TimesLIVE *article 'Paul O'Sullivan apologises to Krejcir's Lawyers'*)

10

LOOTING THE SPOILS:
THE ESTATE

Convoluted estates are not that unusual, but the Teazers' group, a legal entity deliberately constructed to confound SARS, was another matter altogether. Adding to the complexity was the shock, the emotional turmoil and confusion inherent in a situation where the head of the company, a father and a husband, had been murdered. The estate was more than the vast and complicated business empire; it also included numerous properties, trusts, insurance policies, and a garage full of supercars.

Lolly's estate needed a bit of tidying before it was subjected to any official scrutiny, and the urgency with which various parties became involved in the dealings of the company immediately following Lolly's murder was far beyond the usual efforts of a family trying to secure their inheritance. Lolly's tax lawyer, Alan Allschwang, began sending emails at 6.00 am on the morning of Lolly Jackson's funeral. Alan's main objective was to minimise the threat to the estate from SARS. Among his first instructions was a request to Ricardo to gather all the vehicle registration documents so that Alan could verify them for legitimacy. (Lolly had a habit of registering vehicles in others' names as a tax dodge.) We were alerted by the media that SARS was about to appraise the vehicles, which left the lawyer in a heightened state of anxiety.

Over the next 20 minutes, emails flew from Alan's computer, expediting matters relating to the various companies and their asset holdings. He also requested a list of the life insurance policies that Ricardo was supposed to have had in his possession. SARS was Alan's main concern and his intention was to inject cash into the Teazers group's tax liability.

While Lolly's family, friends and staff were mourning his loss and contending with our grief, Alan was liaising with the tax authority, assuring them that while the executors had yet to be confirmed, he would be handling the estate in the interim. He promised that Teazers was willing to submit in terms of both the group's and Lolly's personal liability.

However, Alan's dealings with SARS were hampered as he needed to obtain power of attorney, and there was a distinct lack of financials from the past two years – either due to Ricardo's alleged misplacing of them or as a result of Lolly's intense hatred for SARS and his reluctance to cooperate in any way with this particular form of officialdom.

I became involved in the estate because Ricardo had been effectively removed from all business-related affairs. Alan needed me as I was the only staff member left in the office with any institutional memory and understanding of the history of Teazers. Robyn had resigned and Ricardo had been arrested. Demi was unaware of all the intricacies of the estate and she needed someone she could trust to guide her through the complex maze. I was responsible for locating the necessary documents and supplying Alan with any information he required. Initially, the idea of being elevated to a position of trust and need appealed to me immensely. It provided me with a sense of security which I craved. The first week in my new 'role' revolved around matters pertaining to Ricardo – what he owned, how much it cost and who he owed money to. Alan requested a plethora of information and conducted exhaustive research into Ricardo's businesses, bonds and his fiancée Nichol's affairs. However, the focus soon shifted to matters relating to Lolly's estate.

According to the will that was submitted to the Master of the High Court for approval, First National Bank (FNB) was nominated as an executor of the estate. However, the will also included a suspensive clause that allowed Demi the right of veto, as well as final say in all incidents involving potential disagreements. FNB refused to accept these conditions and tendered their resignation as executor to Alan who, by all accounts, seemed pleased to accept it. Alan then brought Sanlam on board as an executor and they set about completing the usual tasks of creating an inventory of all assets of the deceased estate, ensuring that all valuations were in order and drawing up liquidation and distribution accounts (*see Appendix 8 on page 240*).

The sheer scope and spectrum of the company's assets and shares was overwhelming. It required a Herculean effort to update and research the entire group's portfolio. As things stood, Lolly's business holdings consisted of eight operating companies, four property companies, eight sundry companies and five trusts. There was also a total of 21 dormant entities.

It would transpire that some businesses had been sold in order to dispose of a property they held, some owned assets and could not be considered dormant, while others still owned no assets and had to be put into dormancy. This resulted in certain entities being unable to fulfil the requirements stipulated in terms of payments and bequests.

The logic behind such a convoluted arrangement was clearly Lolly's own. For example, he would often establish two companies to operate a single branch of Teazers: there was for example, Teazers Boksburg cc and Boksburg Teazers cc. This was set up not only for tax purposes – Lolly could explain away the similarity in company name and submit the lesser tax return – but also so that, if at any stage Lolly needed to side-step a creditor, he could place one close corporation into liquidation while the other would continue to exist, and trading could continue uninterrupted.

To add to the complexity, there was no official 'head office' so to speak, and each company simply flowed into the next, devoid of any hierarchical structure. Such an arrangement was manageable only as long as Lolly remained at the helm. While this strategy succeeded in confounding the tax authorities, it quickly became a massive encumbrance that burdened the companies' inheritors. Other than Lolly, Ricardo, now out of the picture, was the only person who could unravel the corporate web.

In the interests of simplifying matters, Alan made a unilateral decision that Teazers Restaurant (Pty) Ltd would become the corporate head office. Interestingly, this particular company was inactive, a parking lot being its only asset. The consequence of this change was that Demi, who had inherited this company – was now positioned to be in complete control of both the group and the capital that flowed through it, as opposed to her previous share within each branch.

Inevitably, change followed. 'Head office' staff, myself included, would no longer be paid by a specific branch and we would now draw our salaries from this central entity. The individual branches were also instructed to begin paying a franchise fee to the corporate head office. This would permit the use of the Teazers' name and would include 'the expenses of advertising, group marketing etc', a rather vague and open-ended description. The idea behind this strategy was to boost Teazers Restaurant (Pty) Ltd's balance sheet, but it would also go a long way towards creating the perception that this corporate head office ran all the individual branches.

Once the logistics were in place, the process of deregistering Lolly from all the companies and replacing him with the executors began. CIPRO (Companies and Intellectual Property Registration Office) forms now had to be signed by all the partners, but some refused to do so until they had considered their legal positions. Finalising CIPRO's requirements took four months to complete.

On 1 July 2010, I awoke to a headline in *The Star* boldly claiming: 'Plenty of Lolly in Jackson's Estate.' (*scan QR code 12 on page 219 to access IOL article*) Horrified, I called Demi and she asked me to contact Alan urgently and ask for advice. He was, by contrast, utterly calm and felt that this was an ideal vehicle to demonstrate to SARS that there was more than enough value in the estate to satisfy the tax authority. He even asserted that he would send SARS a copy of the article himself. Demi, however, was displeased that aspects of her personal life were now available for public consumption. It later came to light that *The Star* had obtained a copy of the will from the Master's office and had quite astutely dissected its contents.

Around this time Alan asked me to meet with a friend in order to sell off some of the memorabilia from the Rivonia branch, which the woman would in turn sell on at a profit. At the time that Lolly had been confronting tax issues, Alan had informed SARS that Lolly had overcapitalised on these items and that their value had steadily declined. Alan now therefore wished to dispose of the items for as little as possible to lend credence to his statement to SARS. When the offer came through it stated:

> As I explained to you the market for memorabilia is very depressed at the moment, and most of the items will need to be reframed. The other problem is that there are no certificates of authenticity and buyers are very fussy.

She offered the princely sum of R25 000 for the following items:

a) *Guitars – ZZ Top; R Stones; Queen; UB 40; B Adams; Kiss 'Ace Frehley'; Offspring; Jamiroquai; Guns 'n Roses; E Clapton*

b) *Sporting memorabilia – Mike Tyson glove; Pierfrancesco Chili Visor; Moto GP Picture*

c) *CDs – ZZ Top; M Jackson; Commitments; Meat Loaf; T Turner; Sting; Cocker*

d) *Tony Montana Dollar*

Unknown to Alan and his friend, I had previously had the items valued by a reputable agent. He'd placed the total at R234 000, without certificates, adding that these were local rates and, if sold internationally, we could expect a lot more. I urgently contacted Demi, against Alan's express wishes, and advised her not to proceed with the sale. On this rare occasion Paul De Jager actually agreed with me and we decided to see how things would play out. Paul would arrange a counter-offer of R50 000 to see what would transpire. Alan's friend felt the amount was too high and withdrew her offer. An unhappy Alan conceded that a higher offer would be better and left the issue alone. Paul never actually followed through with the deal and the memorabilia can still be viewed in various Gauteng-based branches. While I derived a certain satisfaction from derailing Alan's project, I knew that he would exact revenge at some future point.

The next matter to be dealt with was the dividend payments, the first of which had to be made to the family within three months of Lolly's death, or they would lapse indefinitely. A third concern was that we had to determine which payments could actually be made as some of the companies no longer existed. The resolution was that Demi, Samantha and Manoli were each to receive a monthly amount which would be paid out over the next five years, and although Manoli was to receive the lion's share, Demi ensured that it all evened out by diverting some money towards Samantha. (She was taking cash from the business as well as drawing a salary.)

By now, Manoli was no longer working for the group. Apparently, just after Lolly's death, he had conducted an interview with potential dancers in the changeroom and had ordered them to strip completely (Lolly had always let them retain their G-strings), which had caused them much embarrassment. Demi found this unacceptable and had instructed him to 'take a break' – meaning he was no longer considered a part of Teazers.

Next, Alan had to dispose of Lolly's cars and he offered Manoli his pick as part of his share of the estate. Manoli opted for a yellow Porsche 911 Turbo, a sentimental choice that pleased Alan as not only were there other far more expensive and exclusive vehicles available, but as the lawyer intended to sell the cars as a collection, the slightly dated German supercar would have detracted from the other exotics.

When it came time to legalise the new ownership of the car, it transpired that in a typical move to avoid tax, Lolly had registered it in the name of an ex-girlfriend of his incarcerated brother, Michael. Manoli wasn't the only one benefitting from Alan's desire to offload the vehicles. Paul De Jager caught wind of a Dodge Viper that was being offered to Justin Divaris, the owner of several auto dealerships. The asking price for the Dodge was laughable, so Paul put in a counter-offer for R150 000. Justin didn't want to pay more than this and so Paul won the bid.

Within weeks of Lolly's death, I got a call from Demi. She'd been ordered by Alan to get the Pagani Zonda off the Kyalami property as he'd heard from a contact that SARS was about to attach it. I was told by Alan to go to the house and help Piero (from Rosso Sport Auto) move the vehicle. Alan's instruction was that once the car was loaded onto the flatbed trailer, Piero was to remove the bonnet or some other large part when it arrived at his shop, nearby. This would result in a form of lien over the car and therefore SARS wouldn't be able to follow through with their attachment. Piero did as he was told and after he and a helper loaded the car, he placed a cover over the Zonda so no one would see what was being moved. This would also slow down SARS in their search for the highly desirable vehicle.

In August 2010, I was tasked with working together with Jaap du Toit, an evaluator whom Alan and Sanlam had retained to determine the worth of all the houses. Jaap would also visit Demi and take an inventory of the Kyalami house, cars and assets. Interestingly, when I accompanied Jaap to the Hartbeespoort house, Demi asked me not to allow him to include the barge, two quad bikes and two of the jet skis, as she had bought these with her own money. Alan informed me that they had to be placed on the list regardless but Jaap did as I instructed.

I was never privy to the findings of the evaluations, but do recall Alan telling me that Jaap was to use a high-low valuation. Alan felt that if he approached the Master of the Court with both, they would accept any offer above the low. I'm convinced that numerous items of great value were not present on the list, through no fault of Jaap's.

Manoli, for example, simply claimed Lolly's gold crucifix and chain, as well as his gold Breitling watch from the murder scene. In addition, Demi asked me whether I knew of anyone who might want to buy Lolly's three other Breitling watches which she'd been keeping in her safe. I set her up with a reputable dealer. The watches were Bentley Continentals (and had reference numbers to prove they formed part of a limited edition). Two of them were covered in diamonds from face to strap and back again. The dealer explained that there had been a dip in the market and that this type of watch would only appeal to a very specific buyer and so the watches were collected and returned to Demi's safe.

It wasn't long before the issue of insurances raised its ugly head. Lolly had had all his cars, houses and businesses dependably covered by Rob Sylvester at Econorisk. Alan felt, mistakenly as it turned out, that the cars had been double-insured, and the houses and businesses over-insured as the broker had been trying to earn extra commission. With immediate effect, Alan arranged for the group called Bull and Bear, who were conveniently situated in the same building as his offices, to draw up documents and take over the insurance policies. So sadly Rob, one of Lolly's trusted suppliers who had served him well for years, was replaced. And he wasn't the only one to go. In the coming months, virtually everyone Lolly had dealt with in the past would be replaced (by both Alan and Paul). It appeared that loyalty to the new order was uppermost on the agenda.

By mid-September, yet another complication came to the fore. Alan had grown weary of Shaun Russouw of the Durban club not paying his requisite fees to Teazers (Pty) Ltd. To exacerbate the situation, shortly after Lolly's death Shaun had changed to a different bank account – this meant that Teazers head office no longer had access to the revenues from this branch. This act of rebellion was met with much anger and Alan asked me to email Shaun to inform him that SARS was not pleased with the situation as it smacked of money laundering. Truthfully, the tax authority was not yet privy to this knowledge until Alan contacted the SARS team leader for debt management and national investigations, Ilse Pires. She called me shortly thereafter with the objective of putting additional pressure on Shaun. True to form, Shaun would not give in as he believed the business was his and that Teazers (Pty) Ltd had no rights or titles over it.

At the same time as this 'turf war' was taking place, the sale of 48A Arbroath Road – the house that had been promised to me – was well under way. I'd maintained my composure until now, but the anger and frustration I felt over this suddenly overwhelmed me, and I wrote a carefully worded letter to Alan explaining my position, detailing the promised deals, the double-dealing. I explained that:

> I have sat back and let my life be taken control of and lost out totally in the process...
>
> I feel that Demi is not the one at fault here as she has not got sufficient information at hand to know what the entire story is and therefore what the best way forward is. I therefore am requesting a sit down together including Demi so that once and for all we can get this finalised. Either way this needs to be dealt with.
>
> All I have ever wanted is a straight answer and this is the one thing that seems to elude me.

Everything that had been promised to me had been taken away; even the business Lolly and I were in the process of establishing in the garage area next to Teazers Rivonia. I'd reached saturation point and was tired of all the bullshit. Alan's curt response stood in stark contrast to every promise he'd made to me:

> I am available to meet to discuss this if Demi so requires and I await her further instructions in this regard. As I have no instructions concerning this matter, I am unable to respond ad seriatim to your below mail. Please discuss the possibility of setting up a meeting with Demi at my offices to discuss the matter.

I did as Alan had instructed and met with him, only to be informed that I'd been played, my loyalty preyed upon until I was no longer of value – in short I'd been fucked. I walked out of the building distraught, demoralised and uncertain of what my future held.

⊙

I wasn't the only one upset with the way things were being run. Radovan had also reached the end of his tether and was demanding roughly R9 million in loans allegedly owed to him be paid immediately. Radovan had had enough empty promises. Demi and I asked Alan how best to handle the situation and the lawyer responded: 'The loans are not due – also he must not deal with Sean on this – I suggest he asks an attorney to assist him to lodge a claim setting out amounts he claims are owing and how much he says has been paid (do not let on that we have proof of what was paid).' The last line referred to a file that Lolly and Ricardo had kept, allegedly outlining how much had been paid to Radovan and what was still outstanding. The whereabouts of this file are currently unknown.

My salary was a point of contention and Radovan's outstanding claims were being ignored. Demi said that she had made a large payment towards the running of the estate within weeks of Lolly's passing. Alan, on the other hand, claimed to only have received a paltry R10 000 retainer and assured us that he was doing his job out of love for Lolly. This 'love', however, didn't stop him from sending a bill for approximately R300 000 to Demi in October 2010, which had her foaming at the mouth. Demi approached Samantha Jackson, who was known for her feisty temperament, to question this invoice. It didn't take long before Samantha had caused enough turmoil for Alan to threaten to withdraw from acting for the estate. The matter was eventually resolved but Demi had also taken a monumental risk as Alan had previously brought R9 million of Lolly's investments back into the country from offshore accounts, and had persuaded the South African Reserve Bank to allow him to place the money in an Investec trust account which he now held under his control.

Before long, the Radovan 'loan' saga emerged yet again. Out of desperation, I emailed Alan asking him to please take ownership of the matter and he responded:

> I have no records of any transactions concluded between any Teazers' entities and Mr K – there are certain loan agreements between Mr K and Super Car Café but the due dates for payment are still two years hence (and it appears as if much has been paid).

I did my best to explain it saying:

> The fact of the matter is that no matter what the situation is I am certain that this is something that should be handled by you and not Demi, unfortunately this particular matter is placing huge amounts of stress on her and she is near cracking point. So much so that I went in my personal capacity to ask them to back off of her last week. It is a matter that should be handled by counsel as she has not got the authority to tell them what kind of deal, if any, let alone what the process should be. They are pushing harder and harder each and every day and I am afraid to say that this is not something that can be left alone.

And his response:

> The way I see it Mr K either has a claim against Teazers or he does not – if he has a claim he will need to provide documentary evidence of same – as I have stated above, this matter must be handled by Mr Jordaan.

I continued:

> Please could you contact either one of them on the
> following numbers and set up a meeting so that this issue
> can finally be done away with as there comes a point where
> enough is enough. We are no longer able to concentrate
> on the business at hand as the emotional stress placed on
> Demi is beyond belief. Please I am imploring you to just
> hand[le] this for her.
>
> I have explained that it is not her that makes the
> decisions but rather that as a co-executor something that
> needs to be discussed with the kids and Sanlam as well it
> has to all be taken on legal advice. Please respond ASAP
> as to how we manage the situation.

His curt response:

> Please refer Mr K to Mr Jordaan – I have already provided
> Mr Jordaan with copies of all the documents I have.

The Radovan claim had now fallen squarely into the lap
of Ian Jordaan, who was expected to deal with it without
proper access to the pertinent information (and no
knowledge of the underhand games that were being played).
I would soon come to identify this as a characteristic of
dealings concerning the estate – those involved would hand
over responsibility to another as soon as the seas got rough.
Now running the gauntlet on Demi's behalf was old friend
and First National Bank employee, Mike Hatton-Jones. He
sent an email to Radovan's accountant, Ivan Savov, asking
him to cut Demi some slack, and assuring him he'd unravel
the mystery of the loan agreement. Ivan's response was to
the point:

Hi Mike,

Thanks for your email, however I have been tasked to try and sort out repayment of these loans as I also need to make a living.

Since I started this, we have been told to speak to Alan, to Sanlam, to Sean, to Ian, to Demi. We just keep going in circles.

Radovan is being patient, but Lolly had signed an agreement with Radovan and had also verbally agreed to sort out repayment by end of July 2010.

My client is losing a lot of income by way of interest which is not correct.

The amounts owing are as follows:-
Super Car Cafe:
05/10/09 - USD 200 000 * 7.56 = 1 512 000
14/10/09 - USD 200 000 * 7.52 = 1 450 000
02/11/09 - USD 150 000 * 7.85 = 1 177 500
25/11/09 - USD 200 000 * 7.33 = 1 466 000
22/12/09 - USD 150 000 * 7.74 = 1 161 000
- USD 100 000 * 7.60 =   760 000
Sub Total: 7 526 500
Group Two Investments:
- ZAR6 600 000 – 5 000 000 = 1 600 000
Total: 9 126 500

Radovan is looking to Demi, as his friend, to assist him in coming to some arrangement to repay the monies owed.

Regards,
Ivan Savov

The burden of responsibility now sat squarely on Ian Jordaan's shoulders. The estate's cars had been grouped together and sold for laughable amounts, the houses were standing empty and the pillaging simply continued. Demi would later claim that she'd moved the handling of the estate to a new firm of attorneys because 'everyone was just in it for themselves'. By January 2011, I'd served my purpose and was cut off from any information relating to the estate. Tyrel would henceforth be handling Demi's day-to-day affairs. For me, the era that had moulded me through times of joy, adversity and great sorrow was drawing to a close.

The question remains unanswered: where did it all go?

Sean Newman and Ricardo Fabre at 25 Joan Hunter Avenue, Edleen, Kempton Park – the scene of the murder. The silver sedan in which Joey Mabasa spoke to Sean is parked in the driveway. ©Neil McCartney, The Citizen

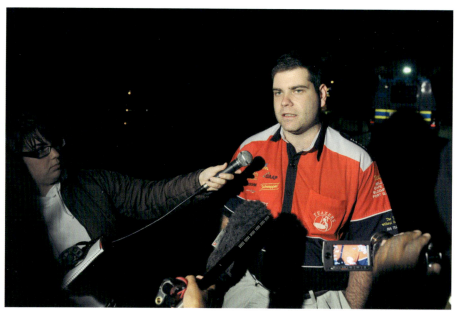

Sean Newman makes a brief statement to the press outside the murder scene. Mandy Wiener can be seen holding her microphone up for comment on the left hand side. ©Neil McCartney, The Citizen

A police van outside the Edleen house while officers scour the scene inside for clues. ©*Neil McCartney,* The Citizen

Lolly Jackson's final resting place in Elspark Cemetery, Germiston. ©*Neil McCartney,* The Citizen

In true Lolly style, the family chose a stretch Hummer to transport them to and from the funeral and burial. ©Neil McCartney, The Citizen

A gust of wind knocks over and shatters an oversized portrait of Lolly that was standing next to his grave. ©Neil McCartney, The Citizen

Family and friends led by Lolly's son Manoli (right) and brother Costa (left) carry his coffin to his final resting place. ©Neil McCartney, The Citizen

Radovan Krejcir seen speaking on his cellphone during Lolly's burial. ©Neil McCartney, The Citizen

Demi Jackson grieves. ©*Neil McCartney,* The Citizen

Lacksom Makhalina carries the shattered portrait of his boss away from the grave site. Ricardo, Robyn and Nichol chat in the background.
©*Neil McCartney,* The Citizen

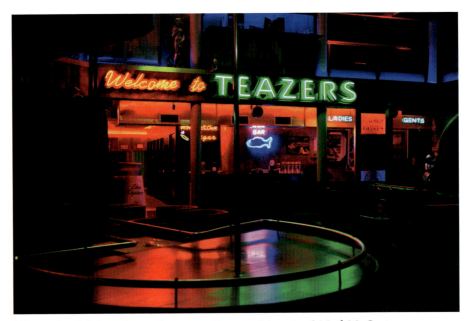

The main club interior and stage at Teazers Rivonia. ©*Neil McCartney,* The Citizen

Lolly headlines on a poster in one of the booths at Teazers Rivonia. ©*Neil McCartney,* The Citizen

A controversial Teazers' billboard, getting mileage from the ANC Women's League. ©Neil McCartney, The Citizen

Lolly stands proudly next to his Lamborghini Gallardo outside his Kloof Road house after being caught speeding at 249 km/h in July 2005. ©The Star

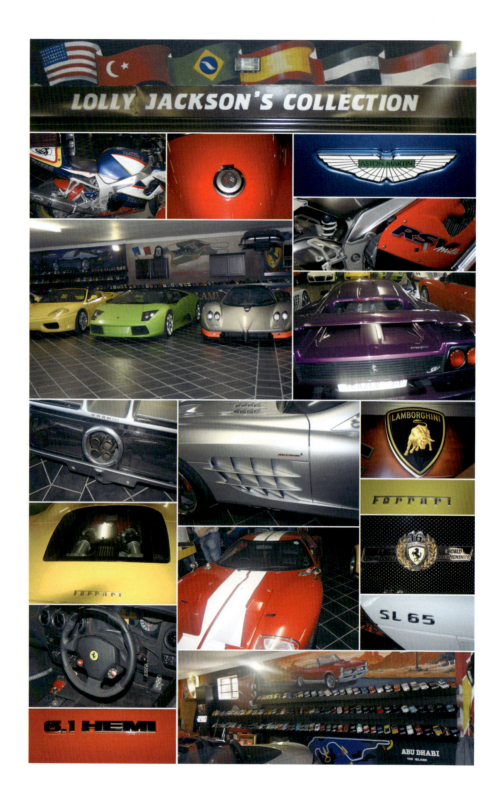

LOLLY JACKSON'S COLLECTION

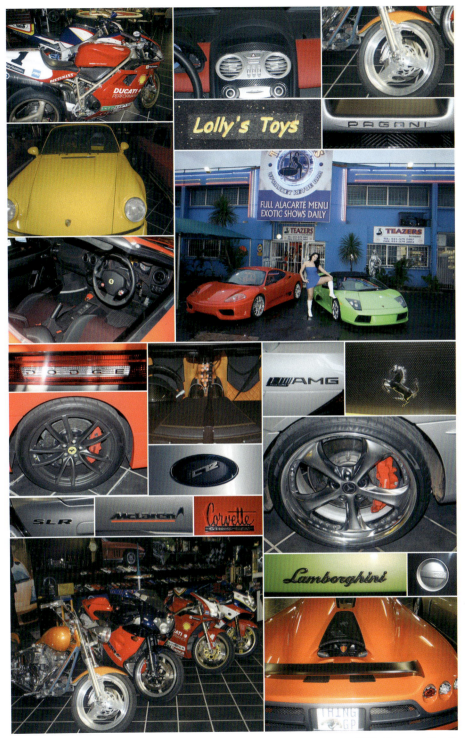

©The Russouw Family

Lolly looking like a proud father as he shows off the newly wrapped Pagani Zonda – originally silver. ©Sean Newman

Friends, including Radovan Krejcir and his wife, play a few rounds of poker in the garage at Lolly's birthday party. ©The Russouw Family

Lolly and his lawyer Ian Jordaan drive away from court after Lolly's release on R5 000 bail in March 2010 – Ian's body would later be found burned on the top of this very car. ©*Mujahid Safodien,* The Star

Paul De Jager, Demi Jackson and Sean Newman speak to Melody Brandon of The Citizen *about the Ricardo Fabre case.* ©*Neil McCartney,* The Citizen

Lolly gives his trademark thumbs-up while speaking to his tax attorney Alan Allschwang. ©*Shayne Robinson,* The Star

PART II

11

SARS:
TAX AND DEATH

Lolly Jackson hated SARS – almost to the point of his own financial annihilation. His intense animosity towards tax authorities was well documented. In his 2006 biography, *Stripped: King of Tease* by Vincent Marino, he claimed that SARS 'bastards' were so desperate to strip him of his cash that officials chased the ambulance taking him to hospital after he suffered a heart attack in 1999. According to Lolly, his heart problem flared up while he was on a holiday in Greece with Demi. When he was flown back to South Africa on what he described as an emergency medical flight, he said that SARS officials were waiting for him – and followed him all the way to Milpark Hospital.

'They were not letting me out of their sight. They wanted

me dead or alive and all the millions I had stashed away,' Lolly claimed, before describing how he nearly died in the hospital's emergency room. 'The first people I saw standing in the passageway were the people from SARS. All I could think about was death and taxes, the bastards!'

'SARS slips up'

Lolly claimed that his 1999 tax problems were the result of a 'mistake' made by SARS and by his hiring a new accountant 'which had caused a few hiccups'. SARS did not appear convinced by the explanation. In 2001, tax authorities obtained a writ of execution against Jackson. The document allowed SARS to attach Lolly's property to pay tax debts estimated at over R8 million. Lolly was adamant: the tax man was wrong. He said that SARS had mistakenly claimed R12 million from him because he was using his personal Prestige bank account to hold monies collected from his various Teazers' branches purely in order to avoid bank fees.

'This may have looked like "kite flying" [moving money from one account to another, and back again], thereby inflating the money in each account, but it was not,' Lolly stated in his biography. 'I was playing with money and using the system to my advantage. Unfortunately, the Prestige account was in my personal name and all this cash must have looked like personal income.' Lolly claimed that SARS had admitted the error and had reassessed its tax claim against him at R1.7 million. He said he was issued with a certificate 'confirming that SARS had finalised their investigation and that all income tax and VAT had been paid' on 15 May 2003.

But Lolly's tax problems were clearly far from over.

He evidently tried very hard to disguise the extent of his problems with the tax man. Constrained by the privacy provisions of the Income Tax Act, SARS has never commented publicly on its long-standing war with Lolly. He was quoted in newspaper articles about SARS raids on Teazers in December 2008, claiming that SARS must have its figures 'screwed up', as he regularly paid taxes.

He was quoted in *The Star* as saying that SARS claimed he owed them R400 million in outstanding tax following a 2005 tax audit. He said this was absurd since a tax assessment of that magnitude would indicate an annual turnover of R4 billion. Lolly claimed that this dispute was being dealt with through an Alternative Dispute Resolution (ADR) hearing set down for January 2009. SARS spokesman Adrian Lackey told *The Star* that SARS would never have seized Teazers' assets if a date for an ADR hearing had already been set, suggesting that the assets were seized in relation to 'another type of tax'.

Ducking and diving

Dozens of emails between SARS officials and Lolly's lawyers in the year before his murder vividly illustrate the full extent of the tax crisis in which he found himself. Lolly's legal strategy with SARS, it would later appear, was to admit that his businesses were not fully tax compliant. But he would delay legal action against himself and Teazers by resorting to ADR and then haggling over the terms of his eventual settlement with the revenue service, disputing the finer details of the claim against him and debating exactly what amount he needed to pay back. This apparent avoidance strategy could, however, only work for so long.

Correspondence from February 2009 shows that Lolly's lawyers were desperately trying to stop SARS from selling the Durban Teazers branch in order to meet tax debts. But, despite numerous threats, SARS never sold any of Lolly's assets.

In March 2009, SARS dismissed Lolly's claims that he had obtained a R7 million loan in 2004 from Mark Froman, the owner of sweet company Cartoon Candy. Officials claimed they had contacted Froman for details about the loan, but that he had 'denied having lent the sum of R7 million to the taxpayer and instead advised SARS that the taxpayer invested R9.5 million in the property known as Starr Polkinghorne during the 2004 tax year'.

As a result, SARS disallowed the loan and instead recognised the R9.5 million as an 'asset... in the hands of the taxpayer'. SARS was convinced that Lolly had used false loan claims to dramatically under-declare his taxable income. And he did not have the documentation to prove them wrong.

Alan Allschwang didn't mince his words in response to SARS's Froman claims, telling his client that he would be wasting his time and money if he attempted to challenge them 'unless you are able to demonstrate conclusively that Mr Froman has acted untruthfully'. Allschwang further advised Lolly not to fight SARS on its personal tax claim against him, but rather to work out a settlement plan in terms of which he would pay them. Lolly would later tell SARS officials that he had repaid Froman in 2008 'as part of the settlement of a litigious dispute'.

According to SARS: 'The taxpayer believes that Mr Froman, having found himself on the "wrong side" of the litigation, was less than delighted by the outcome. Not unsurprisingly, as far as the taxpayer is concerned, when Mr Froman was contacted by SARS to verify the loan to the taxpayer, he denied the existence of same. On the strength of this investigation, SARS disallowed the taxpayer's objection.'

SARS was, however, careful to note that it was not alleging that Lolly's action 'constitute[d] intentional tax evasion or fraud'. In the months following Lolly's murder, tax authorities would nonetheless revise that view.

Gambling with SARS

Correspondence also reveals that Lolly believed money or assets that he'd won while gambling could not be taxed – an argument he was later forced to admit was wrong. He told SARS that he won R125 000 from playing poker in 2004 and R150 000 in 2005.

Ricardo Fabre further reveals that Lolly used arbitrary gambling to 'confuse' SARS. He would bet his cars or motorbikes in bizarre games of chance with his friends and associates, and then tell tax authorities that their assessments of his vehicle assets were wrong because he had lost certain of these cars through gambling. At one stage, says Fabre, most of Lolly's cars were stored in a warehouse. The vehicles' ownership papers would, in fact, be moved far more frequently than the cars themselves.

The cars, however, were not Lolly's greatest or most urgent tax problem. In July 2009, SARS sent Jackson's lawyers notice that it was disallowing his objection against a R5.5 million VAT claim made against the Teazers Midrand restaurant. According to SARS, records it had seized during a June 2008 raid on Jackson's businesses revealed that Lolly had charged 'output VAT' on table and lap dances. 'The VAT was collected and must be accounted to SARS,' three national tax investigators stated in one of many letters to Lolly's attorneys.

While Lolly attempted to use credit card statements, bank deposits and balance sheets to show that he had paid VAT, SARS dismissed his analysis of credit card vouchers as 'incomplete and incoherent'. SARS used turnover reports and cash slips to back up its claims that Lolly had massively underpaid on the VAT he owed. On the same day that its officials dismissed Lolly's challenge to the R5.5 million claim, SARS disallowed his protest against a R6.2 million VAT claim against Teazers Rivonia. The explanation for the refusal was again based on documentation seized by officials during the June 2008 raids on Jackson's businesses, which SARS investigators said clearly showed that 'VAT was charged on the full amount including the dancer's receipts. The VAT was collected and this needs to be paid over to SARS'.

Unimpressed

Allschwang told Lolly that SARS had originally claimed that it had grounds to impose VAT on 'a capital under-declaration' of R519 million at Teazers Midrand. It later reduced that amount to R21 million. He also claimed that tax authorities believed that there had been a similar under-declaration of R121 million at Teazers Rivonia but had reduced the sum to R22 million. This, he argued, was a massive improvement on the tax penalties that the businesses had previously faced. If Lolly was impressed by the reduction, he didn't show it.

Allschwang sent Lolly an email three days after the SARS demand letters were sent, stating that 'the only good news is that the amounts they [SARS] are claiming have come down considerably, and the penalties (although still very high) are lower than anticipated.' Allschwang said he would bring an immediate appeal against the SARS decision to refuse Lolly's challenge to its VAT claims, but told Lolly this appeal was likely to fail but 'we may be successful in reducing the penalties'.

'The simple hard truth,' said Allschwang, 'is that from a legal point of view, if they have till slips confirming that you charged VAT, GAAP is able to demonstrate that the information can be extrapolated from the system, and [if] the banked amounts match the till slips which include the VAT, we are going to have a major difficulty to demonstrate that the amounts you collected for the dancers were treated as non-vatable.'

Demands and settlements

Two days later, Lolly's lawyers reached a settlement with SARS over outstanding VAT and PAYE taxes on his Teazers' restaurants in Pretoria and Midrand. As part of the settlement deal, SARS agreed to reduce its income and VAT tax claims against the businesses by 31.6 per cent. SARS also agreed to reduce its additional tax claims on the businesses from 150 per cent to 15 per cent, but refused to reduce its tax penalties. The Commissioner accepted Lolly's offer of R100 000 for the PAYE he owed for the Teazers Midrand restaurant. SARS then promised to provide Lolly's lawyers with a revised assessment of the restaurants' tax bills within 60 days. Lolly's lawyers promised payment of the revised bills within 30 days.

Just over a week later, SARS issued Lolly with a final demand for payment of taxes owed by him, his Big Name Investments company, Teazers Midrand restaurant and Teazers Comedy and Revue company. SARS wanted a paltry R416.37 in tax from Big Name Investments, R2.9 million from Teazers Comedy and Revue, and R5.8 million from the Teazers Midrand restaurant.

SARS's personal tax claim against Lolly for 2004 to 2007 was the highest of the claims: R10 million. If the amount wasn't paid within seven days, SARS threatened to enter his name in the National Credit Register or attach his property to pay the debt. SARS had strongly suggested to Lolly that he sell one or both of his homes to cover the debt, but Lolly had told tax authorities that the stagnant property market had made doing so nearly impossible.

A week later, Allschwang sent an email to SARS in which he stated that Lolly accepted that he owed the amounts in question and agreed to pay off his tax debts by an amount of R350 000 every month. If SARS believed that this email showed that Lolly was finally willing to make right with the tax man, they were evidently misguided. Lolly's war with the tax man was clearly very far from over.

Plea bargains

On 14 August 2009, attorney Sherouda Novis emailed SARS to plead that Lolly be allowed to hold off on paying his tax debts until Allschwang returned from leave. Novis revealed that SARS was insisting that Lolly immediately pay the full R17.2 million he owed to SARS, a demand that she said 'will demonstrably cripple our client's businesses'. SARS agreed to suspend its demand for payment until 28 August 2009, after Allschwang returned to work.

Two weeks later, Allschwang emailed SARS to confirm that Lolly had paid the R416.37 owed by Big Name Investments, but hadn't paid any of the other outstanding amounts because of various issues connected to the amounts concerned, which he asked the revenue service to either clarify or resolve. He ended the email with: 'I am so sorry to burden you with all this but you will appreciate that I am trying to confine the issues in order to bring this long-standing dispute to an end in the best interests of all.'

The following day, Allschwang sent Lolly an email, urging him to pay 'at least three more cheques of R350 000 on your personal tax liability' to SARS. Doing so, he suggested, might persuade the tax man not to demand that Lolly pay the whole amount he owed.

The lawyer was clearly being placed in an increasingly difficult position by Lolly's extreme reluctance to pay the bulk of the money he owed SARS. That failure would seemingly cloud SARS's eagerness to consider Lolly's objections against the tax debts owed by his businesses.

The day after he sent his email to Lolly, Allschwang sent SARS copies of his client's appeals against taxes imposed on the Teazers Midrand restaurant for 2007 to 2009 and Teazers Rivonia for 2006 to 2008. While Allschwang claimed he had not received SARS's revised assessments of the Teazers' tax debts, SARS pointed out that it had receipts showing that the documents had been faxed to and received by his offices. SARS official Natasha Bruce irritably noted that she had faxed the assessment letters – and copies of their fax receipts – to Allschwang weeks before, 'after the previous time that you claimed not to have received the letters of assessment'.

Bruce went on to state that she would only deal with the collection of Lolly's outstanding tax debt, a large portion of which she said was 'flagrant default' and threatened that 'necessary collection methods' would be used to ensure the payment thereof. She also pointed out that Lolly had yet to provide SARS with a number of tax returns for his businesses. Her letter made it clear: SARS was tired of trying to negotiate with Jackson. Attached to the document was a final demand for the R1.6 million in tax owed by Teazers Rivonia.

The following day, Bruce sent another email to Allschwang. She acknowledged that Lolly had given SARS three cheques for R350 000 each as part of his agreement to settle his tax debts. She said she had received Lolly's request for deferment of his tax payments, but described this request as 'ambiguous' and said that she needed Allschwang to fill in a revised deferment application: 'I requested certain information in order to process your request. Contrary to your "instruction", I did not receive the requested documentation.'

Deals and delays

Bruce wanted Lolly's updated income and expenditure statement, updated assets and liability statement, most recent list of debtors and creditors, and bank statements for the last six months. In another letter emailed on the same day, she described tax returns submitted by Allschwang and Lolly's financial manager Ricardo Fabre as partially 'illegible'. She added that her schedule revealed that Teazers had failed to provide SARS with PAYE, SDL, UIF and VAT returns and 'I will appreciate it if you will deliver the outstanding returns at one time'.

Twenty-four hours later, an obviously angry Bruce again wrote to Allschwang. She accused him of choosing to ignore her previous emails about Lolly's request for deferment of his tax payments. She said that Lolly's request for a delay in the due date of payment couldn't be presented to the relevant SARS committee without the information that tax authorities wanted from him. 'The time given to submit the information has already expired,' she added. Lolly, she said, would have to pay interest on the nearly R20 million he owed until he had paid the full amount. She ended the email with what had become SARS's standard threat: 'The necessary collection action will be taken in order to secure the settlement of the outstanding amounts.'

Allschwang emailed Lolly within a day of receiving Bruce's letter and copied Fabre, urging the financial manager to supply SARS with the information that Bruce wanted. 'As I previously advised, further appeals against his [Lolly's] personal tax bill have a ZERO prospect of success,' he wrote, adding that Lolly's application to delay his tax debt payment – until he managed to sell one or both of his properties – was 'going to be met with stiff resistance'.

In a separate email to Ricardo Fabre he wrote: 'SARS have called me and pointed out that they have pulled records off the NATIS system and determined that Lolly bought a new Merc which was not financed – this is why I recommended that you urgently send through a further series (at least three) post-dated cheques each in the amount of R350k in an attempt to placate them. The bottom line here is that, if it is not already too late, SARS WILL SEND THE SHERIFF TO ATTACH LOLLY'S PERSONAL ASSETS [his emphasis] unless we can get this matter back under control. Please give this matter your immediate attention.'

Auctioning for time

Twelve days later, Allschwang emailed Lolly about his upcoming attempt to auction his luxurious Bedfordview mansion, which had received a large amount of media coverage: 'In terms of the previous undertakings given by you to SARS, you are required to inform them on anticipated disposals/acquisitions that exceed R500k. It is in any event very likely that SARS will be aware of the auction... my strongest advice is to make a full and frank disclosure in advance of the sale and ask them to defer their collection activities until you have concluded the transaction,' he stated, adding that SARS had the legal right to seize property in order to satisfy tax debts. 'In other words, if I were SARS, I would be looking to recover the outstanding tax from the proceeds held by the auctioneer and/or transacting attorney attending to the transfer.'

Allschwang wrote to SARS less than two weeks later,

informing tax officials that Lolly intended to auction off his Bedfordview property. He said that Lolly was 'hopeful that the property will be sold, and that the proceeds so derived will be sufficient to settle the outstanding mortgage bond (R4.2 million) and his personal income tax liability'.

Savile Row Auctions – which was conducting the Bedfordview property sale – was confident that the hype surrounding Lolly's 'Playboy mansion' would translate into eager buyers. Auctioneer Mark Kleynhans told Lolly that the number of people viewing the house was 'very high'. Unfortunately, the publicity failed to translate into the price that Lolly wanted. The highest bid for the mansion was reported as R5.5 million – substantially below the R14 million minimum that Lolly was prepared to accept.

Lolly was quoted in *Beeld* on 5 October 2009 saying that he wasn't 'giving his house away for free and would rather keep it'. And he was well aware that SARS officials would be at the auction to monitor the sale. Unbeknown to the tax man, Lolly was offered R8 million for the property but, knowing that all proceeds of the sale would go to SARS, he turned it down and decided to go the conventional property sale's route. Numerous agents begged Lolly to lower his R14 million asking price. But, when he finally did, every deal he agreed to fell through.

Newspaper reports revealed that, when the bidding for the property was in full swing, Lolly shouted out that he'd also include two exotic dancers. He also appeared eager to undermine any suggestion that the auction was part of an increasingly frantic attempt to generate cash. And, in an aside before the auction that the media interpreted as a joke, he said that he was going to use the money to pay SARS. 'Everybody thinks that you're desperate if you're selling your house at an auction, but I certainly am not,'

Jackson told *Beeld* after the auction. He said he had used the auction platform because it is a popular and easy way to sell property assets.

With the auction having failed to generate the money Lolly needed, Allschwang approached SARS in October 2009, suggesting a new payment plan for his client's outstanding tax. SARS was adamant: it would not agree to any such plan until Lolly had handed over his bank statements, list of debtors and creditors and 'a comprehensive income and expenses statement'.

Unimpressed

SARS was clearly not satisfied with Lolly's response. Two weeks later, Bruce and SARS legal adviser, Gert van Heerden, sent Allschwang a series of questions about Lolly's bond repayments, a trust registered in his name and a mysterious R4.5 million deposited in his Standard Bank Gold Card account on 28 December 2008 and withdrawn the same day. Allschwang responded that the money was 'derived from mortgage bond access facilities' and said he needed more time to get the other answers that SARS sought. But he evidently didn't do that quickly enough.

Gert van Heerden emailed Allschwang a week after his office demanded answers, pointing out that Lolly hadn't provided the information that tax authorities needed. SARS now had even more bad news for Lolly and his lawyers: they had refused his request for a deferment of his tax debt payments. They also raised doubts about whether Lolly had actually paid the instalments he had promised SARS: 'Kindly also note that to date Mr Ricardo Fabre from your client's office has failed to provide our Mrs Bruce with proof of payments as allegedly made by your client, and has cancelled various meetings set up to address the issue on extremely short notice or even after the scheduled meeting. Due to the above, we are placed in a position where we have no other option but to decline the offer of deferred payment arrangements.'

Bruce also expressed her unhappiness with Fabre who, she claimed, had cancelled meetings with her three times in a row because 'according to him, he had other matters of a more critical nature to attend to'.

Lolly was enraged by Fabre's failure to appear at the meetings, demanding to know why he was 'fucking around' with the tax man. Fabre had confirmed the meetings, but had never explained to either Lolly or his staff why he cancelled at the last minute.

Fabre's apparent reluctance to meet with SARS would – with hindsight – become shrouded in suspicion. When the issue of the fraudulent cheques was raised by Lolly's lawyers, Fabre argued that the amount of money they said he had misappropriated had been grossly exaggerated. He added that this was done with Lolly's knowledge and consent – and now cast him as a convenient scapegoat for his late boss's massive tax debts.

Demi would become the primary accuser in the state's criminal case against Fabre. She would also attempt to have the man she once described as her brother sequestrated in the South Gauteng High Court. Fabre had told the court hearing during his bail application that he could barely afford to pay the R10 000 bail. This, said Demi, was clear evidence that Fabre 'has obviously moved the money which he misappropriated'. She wanted to bring an application to have Fabre's car and businesses seized to make sure that the money she claimed he had stolen was paid back. But drafts of her affidavit reveal that Lolly's lawyers were themselves unsure of the amount that Fabre had allegedly misappropriated. This was evidently largely because Lolly had done everything he could to avoid leaving records that SARS could use to ascertain the true state of Teazers' finances.

Crisis deepens
At the height of his tax crisis, Lolly fired Allschwang and appointed attorney George Masha to handle his tax issues. Masha then asked SARS to hold back on collecting the money that Lolly owed them so that he could familiarise himself with his client's complex tax history. Allschwang told SARS that Lolly had denied firing him and claimed that Masha had been brought in to deal with 'other issues'. Lolly's staff, however, insisted that he was axed because Lolly was unhappy with what he perceived to be Allschwang's lack of results.

Fabre picked up Lolly's tax files from Allschwang's offices in January 2010 – less than five months before Lolly was murdered. Masha was paid in cash and, according to Lolly's staff, promised significant results in exchange for that fee. But he failed to deliver. Shortly before his murder, Lolly's staff witnessed him screaming at Masha over his request for more money. Lolly was apparently outraged by the demand because he felt that Masha hadn't offered him any way out of his tax mess that Allschwang hadn't already proposed. He would later apologise for the outburst, but his relationship with Masha never fully recovered.

SARS after Lolly
Allschwang was rehired after Lolly's murder and soon began negotiating with SARS over its claim to Lolly's estate. The

tax man was not deterred by Lolly's murder, and officials seemed more intent than ever on finally obtaining the nearly R20 million that the late strip-club boss owed to SARS.

SARS even appointed senior investigator Johann van Loggerenberg – a member of the team who would later probe the financial affairs of suspended ANC Youth League leader Julius Malema – to look into Lolly's estate. Van Loggerenberg was a seasoned investigator who was obviously unfazed by controversy, having testified in the Jackie Selebi corruption case and having assisted the then-Scorpions with their corruption case against President Jacob Zuma. His involvement in Lolly's tax mess heralded a new phase in SARS's attitude towards Lolly and his businesses: they would soon start investigating Teazers as a nexus point for money laundering and racketeering activities that involved over a dozen businessmen. Teazers, investigators would come to believe, had been a vehicle for organised crime.

Krejcir claims

Allschwang would also be confronted with the consequences of Lolly's dealings with Radovan Krejcir – this was a murky relationship that would eventually result in Krejcir's R14 million claim on Lolly's estate.

Two months after Lolly was gunned down, Krejcir's attorneys sent a letter to Allschwang, making an offer to buy Teazers. Allschwang was not opposed to the prospect of selling the business, but stressed that SARS needed to agree to the sale. He told Krejcir's attorneys that Demi had not confirmed that she would sell Teazers, but he made it clear that 'no agreement in this regard shall come into existence unless same, if any, is reduced to writing and signed by the parties'.

Krejcir's attorneys then sent a second letter, raising questions about the future health of the Teazers' businesses after Lolly's death:

> Whilst our client [Krejcir] does not dispute that Mrs Jackson is capable of conducting the affairs of the various business enterprises, it is trite that the deceased was the driving force behind the business enterprises and that he formed an integral and/or essential part thereof. Our client also is of the view that the current influx of tourists (given the FIFA World Cup event) is not truly representative of the actual performance of the business enterprises.

Krejcir's attorneys went on to refer to a memorandum of understanding they claimed Lolly had concluded with Krejcir prior to his death, in which they maintained that Lolly had agreed to stay on for a year after the Czech purchased Teazers. This was a clear demonstration, they said, of just how much value Lolly brought to the businesses.

'Our client contends that at best for the seller, the market price for the sale assets has been greatly reduced given the death of Mr Jackson,' Krejcir's lawyers said, hinting that the price he had previously offered for Teazers could be decreased even further: 'We are requested to point out that the purchase price may well be adjusted post the due diligence and valuation... We request that some consideration be given hereto particularly in light of the SARS claims that exist...'

'We are informed that Mrs Jackson has discussed the matter of the sale and/or purchase of the sale assets and that she is of the view that the proposal furnished to you is favourable.'

But the sale did not go ahead.

Instead, Allschwang wrote to Van Loggerenberg on 28

July 2010 in response to the SARS investigator's questions about what he called the 'Jackson group'. Allschwang told Van Loggerenberg that he'd been working on establishing which of Jackson's multitude of companies corresponded with the foreign banks, obtaining information about Jackson's imported cars and appointing an auditing company to 'evaluate outstanding compliance issues'.

Cars for cash

Allschwang would soon get to the real point of his letter: asking for SARS's permission to sell two of Lolly's cars – which were, because of apparent customs violations, already of keen interest to the tax man. Allschwang said he wanted to sell a Mercedes-Benz and a Lamborghini, both bought in South Africa and therefore not under suspicion of customs fraud, to settle outstanding finances owing on the cars and to pay SARS. He told Van Loggerenberg that he believed the cars together would fetch R3.5 million.

'I am sure you will appreciate that it would be in the best interests of both the Commissioner and the deceased estate if interest that is not being serviced on vehicle finance agreements is retired as soon as possible and repossessions are averted,' he told Van Loggerenberg.

That same day, Allschwang wrote to the then-executor of Lolly's estate at Sanlam, and provided what he said was a 'heads up' on his strategy with SARS. He wanted to pay off as much of Lolly's tax debt as possible – as soon as possible.

'I want as early as possible to demonstrate the executors' willingness to comply, and to apply all surplus cash towards the payment of assessed tax debts,' he wrote. He revealed that he wanted to use the sale of Lolly's cars to satisfy tax debts owed by five of his companies and had asked SARS for permission to sell the vehicles.

Allschwang met with six SARS officials the following month. Minutes of the meeting reveal that he promised SARS that Teazers would not be sold until the group was tax compliant and controls were in place to stop its current tax problems from recurring. He again encouraged SARS officials to allow the sale of certain of Lolly's cars – rather than his properties – to satisfy his tax debts. SARS agreed. But Allschwang was also careful to tell tax officials that the market for Lolly's luxury sports cars was 'very small' and that 'certain of the vehicles were purely collectable in nature and hardly, if at all, of any utilitarian value'.

Auctioning the cars was an option, he said, that his clients wanted to avoid because they would be charged 'exorbitant prices', and reserve prices on the cars were very unlikely to be met. Instead, he suggested, the cars should be sold as part of a lot to a motor dealer or a car museum, thus ensuring that all the cars were sold and avoiding the prospect that certain of the vehicles would be 'cherry picked' and Lolly's estate 'left holding the lemons'. The lawyer proposed that SARS allow Lolly's estate to sell eleven of his cars as a lot. These cars included three Lamborghinis, the Pagani Zonda and the Koenigsegg Competition Coupe X, as well as a Ferrari 360 Modena, Audi R8, Aston Martin DB9 and Chevrolet Corvette. But, while Allschwang assured SARS that all the cars had been purchased above board, the Zonda and Koenigsegg would soon be the subject of serious investigation.

While Allschwang claimed that the Zonda and Koenigsegg had been bought through a local dealer and hadn't been directly imported by Lolly, he was forced to admit that – should it emerge that no customs duties had been paid on the cars – they could be forfeited. He confirmed to SARS that rumours about the Zonda and Koenigsegg being 'tainted' had placed Lolly's estate 'in an extremely invidious position because until the rumours had been squashed once and for all... the vehicles had no commercial value as no purchaser would "touch" the vehicles on any basis'.

Despite Allschwang's assurances, SARS later found that both the Zonda and Koenigsegg had been illegally imported into South Africa. While the Zonda was valued at €214 500, SARS found that it was 'fraudulently understated at the instance of the deceased to be €120 000'. The revenue service further found that Lolly had falsely claimed that the Koenigsegg was valued at €155 000, when it had in fact cost €650 000. Lolly had also failed to pay customs duties on the cars, leaving them liable to forfeiture.

SARS found that Lolly had justified the massively reduced prices by falsely claiming that the cars were second hand. He would then allegedly use falsified invoices to avoid import duties. Lolly's executors were in no position to disprove the findings but, through Allschwang, they tried to persuade tax authorities that the cars shouldn't be forfeited. Instead, they offered to pay the outstanding customs duties plus interest and a suitable penalty. Allschwang told SARS that the penalties it had previously proposed over the car debacle were 'extraordinarily excessive'. He continued to insist that allowing the cars to be sold as part of a lot was the best way of ensuring that they fetched the best possible price.

Personally indebted
Allschwang also told officials that it would not be possible to submit Lolly's final two outstanding tax returns because he still needed to establish Lolly's credit and debit accounts for each of his businesses. The vast bulk of the money that Lolly's estate owed originated from his personal tax debts, but these were tied up with his very messy business taxes.

Finalising Lolly's personal tax issue, Allschwang said, would inevitably put an end to the SARS saga that surrounded the Teazers' empire. Although Allschwang and Lolly's executors may have bought time from SARS, they knew that they would have to produce the outstanding returns – or face an even greater tax bill.

Frantic emails between Allschwang and Teazers' staff revealed the full extent of the challenge they faced. Fabre had not completed the businesses' last set of financials, meaning that its tax returns for 2009 and 2010 were still outstanding.

SARS had at this stage lodged a claim against Lolly's estate with the Master of the High Court. The tax authority, however, made it clear to Lolly's lawyers that it wanted to settle Lolly's tax debts rather than face the prospect of lengthy and expensive court action. SARS was also aware that attaching Lolly's property and selling it at so-called 'fire-sale prices' would not bring in the money that it needed to satisfy Lolly's debts.

Property huntdown

But tax authorities wanted Lolly's Kloof Road property, his Hartbeespoort house and his Arbroath Road property – where he had once housed half-a-dozen strippers – sold as soon as possible. Officials also told Allschwang that he needed to work on selling the Midrand Teazers' parking lot. The revenue service had also started investigating whether money had been shifted from various Teazers' companies to other businesses as a way of avoiding tax. Teazers Durban owner Shaun Russouw – motivated by his own unhappiness with the handling of Lolly's estate – had diverted the money earned by his branch into another account.

Cashing in

Allschwang's solution was to cash in Lolly's insurance policies, which totalled just over R10 million. He used that money to pay off the bulk of Lolly's R13.5 million personal tax liability. It was clearly a far more effective solution than reimbursing SARS with the proceeds of Lolly's properties as the houses had been on the market for months, but there appeared to be little real drive to ensure they were sold.

Allschwang's decision to pay SARS with Lolly's insurance payouts angered certain of his business partners, who felt the cash should have been used to settle Teazers' tax debts. Allschwang argued that he was responsible for settling Lolly's estate, not resolving the tax issues of businesses that were still running.

It appears that the biggest loser in this arrangement was Lolly's former partner Paul De Jager, who lost out on the R2.4 million insurance payout for Tronic Entertainment. De Jager was promised by Allschwang that he would be made sole owner of Tronic, the Midrand Teazers building and given first option to buy the company that owned the Midrand Teazers parking lot – if he allowed the proceeds of the insurance policy to be paid to SARS. But the promised deal never materialised.

SARS Central Enforcement Agency would later contact Shaun Russouw about his apparent diversion of funds into companies controlled by him. Sean Newman told Russouw that his Durban branch owed the tax man 'massive amounts of tax and VAT and have always intended for income earned by Durban Teazers to be used to pay this bill.'

Sean concluded that: 'All funds unlawfully diverted must be moved as a matter of urgency from your entities back into Teazers Comedy and Revue, and you are requested to provide us with copies of the bank statements from these entities [the companies that money was diverted into] in order for us to give these to SARS as requested.'

Tax dodger

Allschwang was also acutely conscious of the negative publicity potential of Lolly's tax saga. After media reports about Fabre's arrest suggested that Lolly's tax situation was less than agreeable, he immediately fired off an email to Sean, demanding that he counter speculation with claims that Lolly had been more than eager to settle his tax disputes at the time of his murder. He went on to state that Lolly's heirs had 'expressed a strong desire to see that the deceased's good name and reputation with SARS was restored'.

Allschwang also urged SARS not to label Lolly a 'tax dodger' until 'all the facts are known'. But establishing those 'facts' was proving to be difficult. In December 2010, eight months after Lolly's murder, SARS still hadn't received the answers it was after. Allschwang again sent emails to Sean and Demi, asking them to 'urgently' provide the outstanding information.

Again, Lolly's deliberate failure to keep accurate financial records would make this almost impossible.

12

THE RACKET

Within months, however, Lolly was no longer the focal point of SARS's Teazers investigation. A year after Lolly's death, newspaper articles revealed that SARS had taken a 'keen interest' in his tax affairs. But SARS appeared to be far more interested in establishing how Jackson's businesses had allegedly been used as part of a complex racketeering enterprise. And it was becoming increasingly apparent that Jackson had allowed Teazers to be used to launder money for a variety of questionable enterprises.

Radovan Krejcir has never attempted to disguise the fact that he and Lolly were part of a scheme he says was operated by banker Alekos Panayi. But he claims he was unaware of any criminal connotations associated with that enterprise.

He claims that South Africa's 'ridiculous' exchange control regulations had put him in a position where he was vulnerable to Panayi's invitation to participate in the scheme.

Panayi has admitted to helping Lolly launder foreign currency since 2007, and he also claims to be the person who introduced Lolly to George Smith and Krejcir. In an affidavit filed at the South Gauteng High Court on 6 April 2010, Panayi listed transfers totalling millions that he said he undertook for Lolly 'without following the requisite exchange control procedures and without the knowledge or consent of the Reserve Bank or the South African Revenue Service'.

According to Panayi, the first of these transfers took place on 2 August 2007 and was for Lolly's exotic Pagani Zonda, imported from Singapore. Lolly, he said, 'did not wish to pay the full purchase price of the vehicle in South Africa, and wanted to make a substantial payment from an overseas offshore account. I understood that the reason for this was to enable Jackson to under-declare the purchase price of the vehicle to the South African authorities and thus pay less duties on the importation of the Zonda.'

Panayi claimed that it was Lolly who approached him with a proposal that he use his position at Laiki Bank to facilitate money laundering:

'Jackson informed me that he had two off-shore accounts at the Bank of Cyprus and suggested that if I was willing to assist him to transfer funds out of South Africa, he would transfer his bank account from the Bank of Cyprus to Laiki Bank.'

Knowing he would earn commission on any funds deposited at his bank, Panayi apparently agreed and Lolly opened euro- and dollar-based accounts at Laiki Bank: one in his name and another in Demi's. After arranging for the illegal transfer of nearly $40 000 in cash into Lolly's Laiki account, Panayi said that he repeatedly helped him to transfer cash into his offshore account.

'Jackson would provide me with sums of cash (being various amounts, generally in the region of R500 000) which I would collect from his house in Kloof Street, Bedfordview,' he said, adding that Lolly would take the cash from a safe 'behind the picture of an exotic motor vehicle' in his garage.

> *'I would match the amounts given to me by Jackson with South Africans holding off-shore accounts who required access to cash. I would provide the cash to the person requiring same who would thereupon make a back-to-back transfer of the equivalent amount (in euros or dollars) from their off-shore account into one of Jackson's accounts at the Bank of Laiki.*
>
> *'Due to the illicit nature of the transactions I did not retain any documentation in respect thereof... Initially, I would pay the funds received from Jackson to a middleman in Bedfordview who represented a number of private individuals in Zimbabwe who needed South African rands and who held overseas accounts. After I paid the middleman, the Zimbabwean businessmen would effect a transfer into Jackson's off-shore account.'*

Panayi claimed that Jackson initially wanted to use the scheme to build up a reserve of foreign currency in his offshore account 'in order to make payment of an amount towards the purchase price of the Zonda'. He estimated that Lolly transferred over R10 million out of South Africa. But the stakes would become higher in December 2007, when Panayi claimed that George Smith – a member of the Greek Cypriot community whom he knew socially – had introduced him to Krejcir.

According to Panayi's evidence, Krejcir needed Smith, who was Cypriot-born, to front for him by opening a bank account in Cyprus as Krejcir could not do so in his own name. To Panayi he apparently seemed to be a perfect participant in the money-laundering scheme. Panayi said he decided to introduce Krejcir to Lolly so that the Czech could 'help' Lolly transfer money out of the country. 'It was clearly more convenient for Radovan and Jackson to deal with each other directly, without any involvement on my part,' he said. He claimed that he walked away from direct involvement in the money-laundering scheme, leaving Lolly and Krejcir to orchestrate their own cash transfers.

According to Panayi, things went wrong because Lolly incorrectly suspected Krejcir of short-changing him on his currency transactions. According to Krejcir, Lolly initially blamed him for the 'stolen' money but, after he showed him proof of Panayi's wrongdoing, Krejcir claimed that Lolly then turned his ire on the banker. Panayi would claim that Lolly repeatedly beat him and threatened him with violence over the missing money. When Lolly took him to court, Panayi hit back with his damning affidavit – which Lolly never had the chance to answer.

While Lolly's response to Panayi's claims may have been a denial of any wrongdoing, evidence of his involvement in other alleged money-laundering activities would emerge after his death. On the day of his murder, Lolly's cellphone records reveal that he was in contact with Stavros Vzigianakis – the CEO of the medical supply company Surgical Innovations.

When the authors contacted Vzigianakis about his contact with Lolly, he grew audibly agitated and responded with the words, 'No comment'. Lolly's staff would later explain why. Surgical Innovations, accused of re-labelling expired medicine by its own staff, had allegedly been using Teazers as a tool for money laundering. Investigative journalism television show *Carte Blanche* suggested that the company was employing disgraced orthopaedic surgeon Dr Wynne Lieberthal – banned from practicing as a doctor after a series of botched operations led to his being struck from the medical register in 2004. In 2006, he applied for reinstatement which was granted shortly thereafter, and it was at this stage that he began using Surgical Innovations as a preferred supplier for the state hospitals that subsequently employed him.

According to cheque records, Surgical Innovations had occasionally paid up to R40 000 to Teazers for 'entertainment'. But Teazers' staff claim that 'entertainment' was a thinly veiled mechanism by means of which Surgical Innovations paid Lieberthal, as he would pick up his cash from the Teazers' offices.

Although the amount of money involved was probably minimal by Lolly's standards, his apparent willingness to involve his business in such a tacky form of money laundering would be interpreted by certain of Teazers' staff members as clear proof that he had stopped caring about his business.

SARS would evidently see it differently: in its view, Teazers had now become a focal point for organised crime.

13
RADOVAN KREJCIR

Radovan Krejcir has his own distinctive way of dealing with the accusations against him. He laughs at claims that he's a mob boss, an underworld kingpin who has directed the murders of at least three of seven people linked to the Teazers' empire – including Lolly Jackson himself. In between his bouts of laughter, he says the murder claims are 'ridiculous':

'I cannot explain it. This was like a, like a ridiculous. It was like a joke for me. The guy who was very close to me and we met each other every week or twice a week, or even three times a week, now they telling me that I was a suspect. That I kill Lolly. For what? What was the reason? That I don't want to collect my

money that he owes me or that I don't want to buy the Teazers after that, and to have all these difficulties more than one year to get my money back? What is belongs to me, it's joke.'

As bodies pile up around him, Krejcir insists he has become a scapegoat for the murders of Lolly Jackson, German supercar converter Uwe Gemballa, and underworld kingpin Cyril Beeka – and the police's apparent inability to solve them. He admits that he was close friends with Lolly and security boss Beeka. He admits to briefly meeting Gemballa in 1995 at a car expo in Prague, whose killers wrapped his face in duct tape and then sat on his chest as he fought for breath. But he denies having anything to do with the murders of any of these men.

Krejcir has never been reluctant to address the claims against him.

In one of a series of interviews at the Harbour Café in Bedfordview – where he and Lolly would meet at least once a week for booze-fuelled lunches – Krejcir described how he was one of the first people to see Lolly's body shortly after he was killed. He also described the murder scene in graphic detail and suggested scenarios as to how the killing may have played out. Convicted drug dealer Glenn Agliotti, himself no stranger to controversy and one of Krejcir's more recent friends, sat next to Krejcir at the table.

Agliotti evidently believes that Krejcir, like him, has been targeted by investigator Paul O'Sullivan for ulterior purposes and unfairly demonised by a biased media. Krejcir has similar beliefs. He claims that life has been very difficult for him since he was accused of involvement in the murders of both Lolly and Cyril Beeka. 'I don't want to have another friends in this country,' he says, to raucous laughter from

Agliotti, adding, 'and I have the biggest shit because of this relationships.'

Later he would tell *eNews* that he and Beeka had bought two boats and hoped to set up a business that would involve patrolling the East Coast of Africa with the aim of protecting ships against increasingly frequent attacks from Somali pirates.

'I know I've never been involved in this Beeka murder and in the end of the day, Beeka was my friend; very good friend of mine,' he said. 'Two weeks before they assassinate him, I have the last meeting with him at my house, and my wife she prepare for us the breakfast and we were talking about our business, future business…

'For me it was very uncomfortable and I felt very uncomfortable because I couldn't go to his funeral… I hope they will find who is really responsible for this murder and after they will apologise.'

The Hawks have claimed that they found a hit list with Beeka's name on it in Krejcir's house just days after Beeka was gunned down. Krejcir described the hit list claims against him as 'ridiculous': 'I cannot explain howcome this hit list came on the story but clearly for me because we ask the prosecutor to show us this hit list and he never did and they don't want to proceed with this hit list so I know it's just rumours and gossips.'

Amid charges that he is a fraudster who has evaded Czech authorities in his native country and faked cancer to cash in on an insurance policy in South Africa, Krejcir claims that he is the target of a political conspiracy.

Krejcir's lawyers would expose the exact nature of his conspiracy claims when they successfully fought for him to be released on bail for the insurance fraud case against him. The same claims will form the backbone of Krejcir's upcoming second attempt to gain political asylum in South

147

Africa. After he was arrested on an Interpol 'red notice', Krejcir told the Kempton Park Magistrates Court that he was a victim of torture and false arrests orchestrated by the Czech government. These shadowy state forces, he claimed, were behind the 'elimination' of his father.

Krejcir claimed that his troubles began in 2002. Prior to this time, he claimed that he was a successful businessman who, after obtaining a degree in economics, began working in the real estate industry and later acquired a stake in a printing company. According to Krejcir, he used the millions he was making to fund the election campaign of Czech Social Democratic Party candidate Stanislav Gross. Through a middle man, Krejcir says he made a deal with Gross. 'Our agreement was that I would borrow Gross the amount of €2 million, funding his campaign during the election. In return, Gross would hand me control of a petroleum company called CEPRO, in the event that he was elected prime minister of the Czech Republic.'

Krejcir claims the agreement was recorded in a promissory note. He stated in a sworn affidavit that Gross was elected as prime minister of the Czech Republic in 2002, but a basic internet search reveals that Gross only came to power in 2004. Krejcir nevertheless maintains that it was in 2002 that he asked Gross for the company he had been promised:

> *'Gross however informed me that he was not of intent to honour the agreement and indicated that it would be better if I simply handed back the promissory note and let the matter be. I was outraged and threatened to alert the media about his behaviour.*

'During July 2002, I was arrested on trumped-up charges of fraud and detained for a period of seven months during which I was physically and psychologically tortured so as to reveal the whereabouts of the promissory note.

'During the period of my incarceration, my father was questioned as to the whereabouts of the promissory note. He was unable to supply any information in such regard and was abducted and eliminated as a result.'

Media reports reveal that Krejcir's father, Lambert, was abducted in 2002 while his son was in Czech detention. Despite Krejcir's suspicions that his father's disappearance was state-sanctioned, in 2006 Czech police arrested local football-club owner Jaroslav Starka and some of his business associates for the killing.

Police believed that Starka and his partners had kidnapped Lambert in order to force his son to pay debts owed to them, but that the elder Krejcir may have suffered a heart attack during the abduction. Starka was released on bail and the case remains open. Radovan claims that Starka and his associates were working for the Czech government.

Krejcir was released from detention in 2003. Shortly after that, he claims his home was raided and he consequently fled the country for the Slovak Republic in fear of his life. He says he was then approached by two Czech police officers who promised that he would not be arrested if he returned and told authorities where he had hidden the promissory note. He claims that he took the officers at their word, but was wrong to do so.

'I was again arrested and detained for a period in excess of one year. During the period of my detention, there were several attempts on my life,' he stated under oath, suggesting that prison guards had tried to poison his food.

Krejcir was again released. Despite the false arrests and torture he claimed to have suffered, Krejcir said that he didn't give up on his attempts to gain control of CEPRO from Gross. After only one year in office, Gross stepped down following a scandal over the shadowy origins of a loan he had used to buy his flat. His wife was found to have had a business relationship with a brothel owner suspected of insurance fraud and money laundering. Despite his attempts to remain in power, he was forced to resign on 25 April 2005 after his once-intense popularity had sunk to an all-time low. Gross was never criminally charged, but the Czech media continue to question the origin of his wealth.

Krejcir claims that Gross's replacement, Jiri Paroubek, promised to relinquish CEPRO to him once he had handed over the promissory note. He says that he refused to do so until the company had changed hands. This stance resulted in his negotiations with the Czech government coming to an abrupt halt 'and my safety and that of my family was again threatened'.

In a scene reminiscent of an action movie, Krejcir claims that over 20 officers raided his home shortly after his refusal to hand over the IOU. He says that his guard overheard one of the men say he would be killed as soon as he handed the document over. He had no choice, he claims, but to go on the run. He slipped out the back door of his luxury villa in Prague in an escape that made headlines across the Czech Republic. According to Krejcir, 'I went to, and took refuge in the mountains for a period of 14 days. During that time, a number of friends arranged a falsified passport for me, in order to escape the Czech Republic safe and undetected.

'I assumed the falsified identity of Mr Tomiga, and went

from the Czech Republic by bicycle into Poland. From Poland I travelled into the Ukraine by train. From the Ukraine I travelled to Turkey on the Black Sea and onward to Dubai.'

Krejcir met up with his wife and son in Dubai and then flew to the Seychelles, where he rented a house from the president's son. He then started a car-hire company. This idyllic life didn't last long however. According to Krejcir, he became aware that the Czech Secret Service was planning to kill him 'by creating the impression of death by accident or natural causes' as part of an operation dubbed 'LOMIKAR'.

The protection he had once received from the Seychelles police was also becoming increasingly expensive. Krejcir claims that the Seychelles government demanded $4 million in order not to enter into a treaty that would almost certainly ensure his extradition to the Czech Republic.

Krejcir obtained a new passport under the name Julius Egbert Savey and fled the Seychelles for South Africa, he says, to escape certain death at the hands of the Czech government. Czech authorities vehemently deny Krejcir's conspiracy claims. They say Krejcir is part of a vicious Czech crime ring and fled to the Seychelles to avoid facing charges of conspiracy to murder, counterfeiting, tax evasion, extortion and abduction. He was also convicted *in absentia* on charges of tax fraud by the Prague Municipal Court and sentenced to six-and-a-half years in prison. Radovan insists that he is currently appealing his sentence *in absentia* and will win.

Krejcir's past was no secret. His arrest upon arrival in South Africa was the subject of intense media interest. His subsequent battle against extradition and his revelations about how he fled authorities in the Czech Republic and the Seychelles, made for fascinating reading.

Lolly knew all about the claims against Krejcir when his

former advocate Mannie Witz introduced him to the Czech at a Ferrari day. The two would meet again a year later, when Lolly accused Krejcir of stealing his money. They were both evidently embroiled in a money-laundering scheme controlled by banker Alekos Panayi.

'Lolly end up in my house seven o'clock in the morning, when I am sleeping until ten first of all,' Krejcir later claimed. 'So he ring the bell, so nobody let him go inside my house. [In the] afternoon they give me his business card. And I remember I met him like, one year before in the Kyalami so I call him, I say "What, what's happening?" He said, "I need to speak to you very urgent."

'I said, "No problem, come the afternoon to my house, we talk. What about?" "I will explain you." He came to my house afternoon with this Alekos guy, which I wasn't deal with Alekos... I don't know, eight months for example, already.

'He came and he told me, "You owe me money." I said, "What you talking about? I don't know you, brother. I met you one year ago, or one-and-half year ago in Kyalami." "No, you have this transfer with Alekos. Alekos give you my money." I said, "Lolly, relax, my brother. First of all I don't know you. I never have any deal with you, we never had any agreements. Alekos brought me some money, because he steal the money from this account in Cyprus, I never pay him this money."

'Because I took this money, it was like a... different was like 336 000 for example, what he steal from this account. So I said, "This is the papers." I was ready with the papers and everything so I show Lolly in front of this Alekos. I say "Lolly look, this was the transfers I did with this Alekos, this was the money that he gave me. So the reality is now that I don't owe Alekos anything, he doesn't owe me nothing but

I not going to do this thirty-six thousand." I said, "Lolly you must understand, he's your bank manager. I am his client, you are his client, and we never deal together. If you have any complaint, go to your bank manager. If I have any complaint, I am going to my bank manager." He understand this.'

Lolly later sued Panayi for the R1 million he claimed the banker owed him. Panayi retaliated a month before Lolly's murder and filed an affidavit exposing Lolly and Krejcir's involvement in the money-laundering scheme. Krejcir insists that he wasn't concerned by the allegations, despite the damage they could do to his prospects of obtaining asylum in South Africa.

Krejcir claims that his and Lolly's mutual outrage over Panayi's 'theft' of Lolly's money birthed a solid friendship between the two men, fuelled by a shared love of parties, risk, fast cars and chess. He grew visibly animated when he described how he and Lolly would race their sports cars on Sunday mornings, speeding at over 330 km/h along winding Magaliesburg roads:

> *'He's got the balls, this guy, you don't understand… So I was angry because he's old man, so how he can beat me now? So I said, "I don't care if I must kill myself, I must kill, uh… beat him." You know what I mean?*
>
> *'We had a lot of fun together. He was very funny person. I am telling you now he sitting here, he will be the leader of the party. Party man. He made sure his jokes and whatever he say the people just laugh. You know what I mean? He was very good and that's why I like him on all my birthday party and the day my son party, and all the time. I like him next to me because he was actually… Whatever the people say, that he is*

arrogant and bad man, and uh, bad behaviour... in me, with regards to me, it was completely opposite. I have completely different relationship between me and Lolly.

'I had a lot of fun with this guy and I miss him. I miss this guy because to be honest with you, Sunday for me was the breakfast run, you know what I mean? Already, and I had a good friend of mine next to me and up... Luckily I find someone who can race. Not talk. Because talking is cheap.'

Krejcir has rubbished security consultant Paul O'Sullivan's claims that he was attempting to persuade Lolly to turn state witness against Krejcir at the time he died. O'Sullivan has made similar claims about Beeka. He told *eNews* that he approached both men through unidentified intermediaries. Krejcir says the claims are nonsense.

'The Lolly, before he died... if you mention in front of Lolly the Paul O'Sullivan name, he had the goosebumps. He was shaking... Sullivan was his enemy. Lolly hate him with passion. He said he... if you mention this name he just get aggressive, you understand? So what Sullivan is saying is a completely nonsense. Is ridiculous. I wish the Lolly would still be alive, to tell you now, if you mention the uh... the Sullivan name he will fucking take the table, he will turn the table. He hate this guy with passion... he hate this guy. So what the Sullivan is saying is completely nonsense, lies and bullshit.'

O'Sullivan and Krejcir have not been reserved about expressing their strong dislike of each other. Following Krejcir's arrest for fraud, O'Sullivan invited reporters to the Harbour Café and sat at Krejcir's table – telling journalists, with a drink in his hand, that Krejcir would never sit there again.

When he was released, Krejcir agreed to an interview with *eNews* at the same restaurant – and used the chance to publicly goad O'Sullivan.

'So he said to the media that I will never again sit at this table,' he said as he sat down. As he sat down he said he wanted to make sure the table was clean and free of 'cockroaches'. 'So here I am, guys, sitting again at my table. *Salut*, Paul O'Sullivan.' He then proceeded to drink his Czech beer in full view of a TV camera.

He later told *eNews*:

'I never met Paul O'Sullivan; I never see him. I never speak to him except through the phone and I know for a fact, I know a hundred per cent guarantee that this guy is working with the Czech Republic authorities. Actually we have some proof now that he has some three guys from the Czech Republic embassy if he need anything to help him and I can see the motive of Paul O'Sullivan to be involved in this – is just money because they apparently promise him and he sign the agreement with Czech Republic government that if he will bring me back to Czech Republic, they will give him $500 000.'

Radovan also says that in late 2011 O'Sullivan, while on a trip to London, was paid a further €100 000 by the Czech government for his ongoing work in this regard. O'Sullivan has refused to address Krejcir's claims.

After his murder, Lolly's backed-up cellphone address book revealed that he not only had O'Sullivan's domestic cellphone number, but also his international phone number – a contact that O'Sullivan apparently gave to very few people.

Asked about the last time he saw Lolly alive, Krejcir becomes pensive. He says the two men met for their regular lunch at the Harbour Café two or three days before the killing. The Harbour Café was the same venue where George Smith would allegedly later announce that he had killed Lolly. Unusually, Lolly had brought his wife along. Krejcir claims that the couple's marriage was clearly in serious trouble, but says that Lolly claimed Demi was trying to reconcile with him:

> '*He were complaining to me that he was going to divorce the Demi and she is the piece of shit dah, dah, dah... He told me that he wants to fuck off from this country; he's got enough. He told me that he will, uh... in front of the Demi... that he will sort this out, this relationship, with this woman – in front of her.*'

According to Krejcir, Lolly's mood did not improve when Krejcir told him that he had information about his financial manager, Ricardo Fabre.

> '*I told him, "Do you trust Ricardo?" the last time when I met Lolly. "Do you trust Ricardo?" "Yes, I trust him, why?" I said, "Listen, Lolly. I've heard from some people that Ricardo is stealing money from you."*
> '*He was nervous. He say, "No. Ricardo would never steal anything from me." "Listen, I even heard that he open his restaurant from the money that he*

*steal from you." He say, "What restaurant?" I said,
"I don't know, I don't have any further information.
But I am just telling you that I heard he is stealing
from you. Your right-hand man." He said, "Never.
Impossible." You know, he was fighting here, you
know, aggressive. He said no and he asked Demi, "Do
you believe he stealing from me?" She said, "No, I
don't believe he is stealing from you."'*

It was a sombre lunch, says Krejcir – very different from the
light-hearted meals he had shared with Lolly in the past. A
few days later, the man Krejcir had once asked to be his son's
godfather was dead.

Krejcir claims he has no memory of the seven phone calls
made between himself and Smith on the day of the murder
because Smith was 'a drug addict… he call many times a
day'. But he has a very clear recollection of the phone call
he received from Joey Mabasa in the immediate aftermath
of the murder.

*'Mabasa called me and told me, "Listen, can you call
Lolly on his phone?" I said, "Why?" "No, just call
Lolly and tell me if you get a hold of him." I didn't
know what was happening. So I called Lolly, his
phone was off, so I call Mabasa and say, "Listen, his
phone is off." After two hours he call again and say,
"Can you call again, the Lolly?" Or one hour, I don't
remember exactly. So I call Lolly and I say, "No, his
phone is off." It's strange anyway since I never reach
his phone off.'*

At about eight o'clock that night, Krejcir claims that George
Smith arrived at the Harbour Café, where he was drinking

with Beeka and at least four other associates. He says he saw Smith parking a Jeep – later identified as belonging to Lolly.

> *'I was sitting here in the table with another six guys and he came and he said, "I kill Lolly Jackson." You know, George, drugs and all this shit. What are you talking about? He looks normal, nothing, no marks, anything. You know? No fight, whatever. What are you talking about? We laugh at him. He said, "OK, no problem." He went to order the two packets Camel Filter and took them, he left to the car. We was watching him. He was walking through the whole parking, sit in this car, this white Jeep Cherokee, and he left.'*

Shortly after Smith's bizarre announcement and departure, Krejcir says Mabasa arrived.

> *'Mabasa said, "Where is the George?" We was sitting with six friends of mine. And we say, "No, what do you mean, man? We was here and George arrive and he left." He said, "No, George called me and that he wants to see me." I said "For what?" He said, "No, George tell me that he kill Lolly Jackson." "No, he told that to us as well." He said, "No, he told me that he wanted to hand himself over."'*

Mabasa would make similar claims about Smith's 'confession call' within hours of Lolly's murder, throwing himself firmly into the media spotlight that surrounded the killing. Less than two years later, amid growing speculation that he was under criminal investigation, Mabasa would get a golden handshake.

Krejcir admits that his wife and Mabasa's wife had gone into an energy-drinks business together, but he vehemently denies that there was anything untoward in his relationship with the crime intelligence boss:

> *'I met him through him the police. I had some problem with the Russian people here in this country and it was investigated. Some crime intelligence guy, his name was Oscar. This Oscar introduce me with Joe Mabasa... He took me to Joe Mabasa because he said to me his boss wants to talk to me. That's why I was introduced by this guy.'*

He denies that he and Mabasa were ever friends, but says the 'good cop' helped him 'when I have the difficulties in this country, the people came to this country to kidnap me or whatever.'

> *'I just have his service that he... I inform him what's happening around and he try to help me. That's it. No money involved, no nothing.*
>
> *'What the people saying is completely nonsense and what they done to him is the biggest mistake, what they done to him in this country. Joey Mabasa, let me tell you something, is the honest cop. He loves to work as a cop, he work for the government, he will die for the government. It was in his mind all the time.'*

On the night of Lolly's murder, Krejcir claims that he, Beeka and their associates offered to take Mabasa to Smith's rented home. They drove Krejcir's white Porsche to the house, where they gave Mabasa a phone number for the property's owner. He told the man, who owns a Pick n Pay franchise, that he needed to come to the house as soon as possible. The property owner arrived an hour later and opened the garage door.

Krejcir claims that he immediately recognised Lolly's body by the decrepit shoes he was wearing.

> *'I was always saying, "Lolly you're fucking pissing me off – you have money, you fucking always with these old scrap shoes." When I see these shoes out from the distance, I said to myself: it's Lolly.'*

He also revealed that Lolly was half-naked when his body was discovered.

> *'But for me it was strange. How it possible that his jeans were on the half, on the, on the knees. You know? Like somebody want to rape him or something, you know what I mean?'*

Krejcir does not believe that Lolly was killed in the garage where his body was found:

> *'You see the people who went to this house, they said immediately in this house, they said there is like a blood, uh... spot. What happened it was somewhere in a different place, not in the garage... I don't know what is a true or what is a rumours. So they said that somebody, what happened that side in the lounge, they cover Lolly there in the lounge and they pull him with his clothes through the whole house to the garage. Because it was like a spot through the house, the blood spots, to the garage.'*

Krejcir says he didn't try to call Smith after confirming that Lolly was dead because he was 'bloody shocked'. He says subsequently he has repeatedly asked Smith about why he shot Lolly, but maintains that Smith has told him 'not to get involved'.

Krejcir's ambivalent attitude towards Smith is apparent. He talks with evident disgust about Smith's drug addiction, but claims he talks to him every day about returning to South Africa and dealing with the consequences of his actions.

He believes that a strange kismet brought him and Smith together in the cells of the Kempton Park Police Station – and this kept them together.

Krejcir told the *Beeld* newspaper in the months following the murder that Smith was 'the first person I met in South Africa. We got released about the same time and he showed me around and gave me advice where to buy a house.'

When Krejcir arrived in South Africa from the Seychelles in April 2007, he was immediately arrested by police and intelligence agents on an Interpol 'red notice', describing Krejcir as an 'international fugitive' and said he was wanted in the Czech Republic for fraud and conspiracy to commit murder. By the time Smith met him, he had been imprisoned alone in a cell for three months, facing extradition and desperate for company. Smith won Krejcir over by using his connections to arrange a take-away meal delivery to the cell he shared with the Czech. The two men indulged in Surf 'n' Turf and caviar from the nearby Emperors Palace. Krejcir was impressed and immediately employed Smith as a runner.

Krejcir was granted bail by the Kempton Park Regional Court in July 2007. Shortly after that, Smith was also released.

'What was very strange – most of the time we spent together... We've been, most of the time, from my custody or his custody, together in the cell. And even though they send him to Boksburg Prison for four days, they send me to the Modderbee Prison. And that, after fucking four or five days, together again in the same cell in custody in Kempton Park. It was like a, uh, not miracle... it was unbelievable to be honest to you. I don't have explanation until today how is possible that we spent so much time, me and him. Me as a Seychelles citizen in South Africa and him as a Greek, in the same custody together. It's unexplainable.'

Did he ever warn Lolly about George?

'Well, how many times Lolly was fighting with me? I mean not with me but he was complaining to me, "What a piece of shit, this fat fucking, uh, Greek." You know what I mean? But whatever. Next day he came and he tell me George is good, he done this now... He was also up and down the Lolly, you know what I mean? I said to Lolly a couple of times, I said, "How you can deal with these people? I reject him one-and-a-half year ago. These people is unstable. He will promise you something but he will never deliver it to you, you understand? He is talking too much, the word is cheap, you know what I mean? The talking is cheap." So I said, "How you can deal with these people?" He never listen.'

Krejcir says he has no idea why Beeka was murdered (which is still unsolved), but has suggested it may have been gang-related. The killing prompted the Hawks (Directorate for

Priority Crime Investigation) to conduct a highly publicised raid on Krejcir's home, on 22 March 2011, which saw Krejcir's son and bodyguard being cable-tied on national television. Krejcir claims he was aware of the raid three days before it happened and left because he questioned its legitimacy as well as fearing for his personal safety. At the time, the Hawks were adamant that Krejcir was a suspect in Beeka's murder. Hawks' spokesperson McIntosh Polela told reporters that Krejcir was wanted for fraud and murder:

'The fraud relates to a R4.5-million claim he allegedly made for cancer, but obviously he doesn't have cancer. We've been able to establish that. The charge of murder relates to a murder that happened in Cape Town. The information we have is that we got documentation with a list of four people that were allegedly going to be killed and one of them was killed, I believe, yesterday. Inside the house we found documentation with a list of those four individuals.

'The four individuals were Cyril Beeka, who by now we know is dead, Paul O'Sullivan, Dr Marian Tupy – who we have done a deal with in relation to the cancer we talked about – and a prosecutor by the name of Riegel du Toit... The prosecutor has to do with the Gemballa case.

'Obviously it was important for us to get him [Krejcir] behind bars to save the other people who were allegedly going to be killed. The other information we have is that there were three hit men who were going to be brought in from Serbia to do the hit.'

But, when Krejcir was finally brought to court, he was only charged with fraud. And the so-called hit list has never been

163

presented as evidence against Krejcir. Krejcir's wife Katerina would later tell *eNews* that she believed the existence of the list was a total fabrication:

> *'I think it's ridiculous. I actually want to see, they must show the hit list because I want to see what is it and what is on it and if it's written by hand or if it's written on the computer because it doesn't make sense to me at all. It's nonsense for me.'*

According to Katerina, the motive behind the lie was 'just to make a big story, just to make it big you know, just to make my husband big criminal and that's what I think'. Addressing the Hawks' claims that her husband had to be arrested to keep his potential victims safe, she sighs. 'That's so easy to say,' she says, 'They say everything.'

Her husband, she says, is a 'good man, not a criminal'. And she is adamant that, despite the state's claims, he has not faked bladder cancer.

> *'My husband is sick. He was having problems long time ago. He was having blood in his urine. He went under six operations. After these operations, he was suffering a lot. He was having this bag, you know, for the blood to come out. You know this bag is supposed to be after this operation, you know maybe one or two days. He was having it for one month. He was in big pain and under medication... it's bad.'*

She later added that she was worried about her husband's 'psychological troubles' – and the impact that the raid would have on him.

Her son Dennis also told *eNews* that Hawks officers had

threatened him with rape and murder when he told them that his father was in Durban on business. He claims officers physically abused him and his father's bodyguard:

'They started the car and now we went somewhere away into Germiston, some dark area, I didn't really know exactly where it was, and there was this steel gate and the driver just hooted and the gate opened and we went inside into some underground garage. Then the driver got out of the driver seat, opened the taxi door and said, "Okay, get out." So I got out.

'He put me by the pillar and he said, "Tell me where your father is." So I said he told me that he went to Durban for a meeting. He said, "No, you're lying. I will beat you up," but he said it more wrong. He said, "I will fuck you up." Then he said, "I will rape you, I will give you a present that you will remember me for the rest of your life." He left me there on the floor, just in socks, shorts and T-shirt for about one-and-a-half hour. And he kept intimidating me, threatening me and then he said, "Okay, get up"... we got back into the taxi. Then they asked us questions again and then we reversed and then we went back to the house. And then I met the lawyer here and he said okay, I'm free to go.

'I was worried what was going to happen to me because really there was no witnesses, nothing, just this abandoned place. I was cable-tied, I couldn't do anything.

'I believe this is not legal and police should treat you properly and not like criminals. I've got nightmares. Sometimes I feel weak. I vomited a couple of times already. I don't feel really well.'

◉

The Krejcir family's abuse claims are now part of a civil claim against the police. But the Hawks have dismissed Dennis Krejcir's claims as 'absolute tosh'. McIntosh Polela was equally scathing about Katerina Krejcir's suggestions that the so-called hit list had been planted:

> *'The wife was not at the scene when we arrived to Mr Krejcir's home so I don't know [how] she can make allegations that we may have planted that hit list. I mean it's quite rich coming from her because she wasn't there.*
>
> *'As regards to the boy, the allegations that they are making against us are quite laughable. I was there all the time; the boy was never threatened. In fact, I was the one who asked if he wanted to lay on the carpet, if he wanted me to loosen the handcuffs that we put on him, so they're talking absolute tosh.*
>
> *'He's talking absolute tosh, I mean really. It's laughable that they make allegations like that and they didn't take time to immediately report such serious allegations to the police. I think the mother should be doing a good job of raising this son to be a responsible citizen of this country, instead of raising him to be an enemy of the state like his father.'*

While the NPA hasn't charged Krejcir with Beeka's murder, Polela has repeatedly stated that this does not mean he won't be charged for the killing. Speaking outside the court after Krejcir's ultimately successful bail application, he also denied claims that the fraud case against Krejcir was ultimately doomed because of O'Sullivan's involvement in the investigation:

> *'That's absolute tosh. We don't have a civilian leading an investigation. He helped us with material evidence, which was very important to us in relation to the case of murder that we eventually want to bring against Mr Krejcir. Is he going to walk? No, he's reached the end of the road.'*

But Mr Krejcir sees things differently.

According to Krejcir, not once in any of the seven or eight murders he has been accused of being involved in, has he ever been questioned by the police. Nor has there been a request for an interview or any statement. At no time has he not been willing to cooperate, but they have just not approached him on these claims.

He has challenged Paul O'Sullivan through his attorneys to a live broadcast of a lie-detector test. He is even willing to allay O'Sullivan's safety fears by doing his end in Cape Town or Durban while O'Sullivan is in a Johannesburg studio. O'Sullivan has declined the challenge.

Finally, Krejcir says he is changing his name to Mr Banana Peel because 'every man that slips and breaks his leg on a banana peel then it is always going to be Radovan to blame'.

14

WHO KILLED LOLLY JACKSON?

Although Radovan Krejcir's name has been linked in the media to Lolly's death, it is George Smith, aka George Louka, who was identified as Lolly Jackson's killer within hours of the strip-club owner being gunned down, wrapped in a duvet and dragged into the garage of Smith's rented Edleen home. The killing was a cold-blooded execution, performed with slick precision that would ensure that Lolly's death was almost immediate. The crime scene was near pristine.

But the man blamed for the murder appears not to fit the profile of the professional killer. Smith has been at pains to portray himself as a God-fearing family man with a good name in his native Cyprus, a placid father of four who was caught up in something beyond his control. Lolly, by contrast, he depicts as a tax-evading bully who used violence to get what he wanted.

The hints and innuendo Smith has used to explain his part in the killing – which he has previously described as an 'accident' – have yet to provide any explanation for the single-mindedness that seemingly drove whoever took Lolly's life. Smith grabbed headlines when he told the *Sunday Times* in May 2011: 'If I go under, I will not go down alone, a lot of important people will go down with me. I will pay the consequences, but they will as well.'

But, in a subsequent interview for this book, Smith vehemently denied that there was any conspiracy behind the murder. The Hawks unit, which is still investigating the murder, has evidently not taken his word for it.

Smith wasn't a stranger to law-enforcement officials prior to the killing, having been arrested on a series of petty charges related to the alleged fencing operation he and his wife ran from their small East Rand supermarket. Before meeting Radovan Krejcir in the cells of the Kempton Park Police Station in June 2007, Smith was widely regarded as a small-time hoodlum by Johannesburg's Greek community.

'He was ordinary, he was always on the outskirts of the Greek underworld. He was a receiver of stolen property who would pick at the scraps tossed at him by the big-time operators. He never got the cream. Only the crumbs,' one of Smith's former associates later claimed. While Lolly knew Smith, the associate said, initially, 'he wouldn't even greet him'.

But Lolly's attitude towards George was soon to change.

Smith and his wife were arrested on charges of receiving stolen property. The police found unidentified commodities in the couple's shop, which they believed to have been taken from a hijacked truck. Smith's wife successfully applied for bail but he was forced to wait two weeks before he was finally released. It was during this time that Smith met Krejcir in the Kempton Park Police Station cells.

When Smith was finally released, he would agree to plead guilty to receiving stolen property if the charges against his wife were dropped. The Cypriot then reneged on that deal and was facing prosecution at the time of Lolly's murder.

Following his release, Krejcir – who was unable to leave the country – used Smith to look after his business interests in Prague and the Seychelles. The Cypriot, who once resorted to selling stolen property to make ends meet, was now flying across the world on business-class flights, courtesy of Radovan Krejcir. He earned a reliable salary for collecting money and was, according to one of his former friends, 'happy as a pig in shit'.

Smith claims that Krejcir instructed him to open a forex account in Cyprus so that the Czech's mother, billionaire businesswoman Nadedza Krejcirova, could transfer the sum of R100 million to her son.

In addition to providing financial stability, Smith's relationship with Krejcir evidently improved his standing in the Johannesburg underworld. Lolly, who had previously refused even to greet him, was now taking his calls and inviting him to poker games. The two men, who would speak to each other in Greek, could not, however, be described as close friends.

Smith appeared to be willing to say or do almost anything for money and, as Lolly's life spiralled increasingly out of control, this willingness would prove to be increasingly useful.

After his arrest on 27 February 2010 on charges that he'd attempted to extort money from the boyfriend of one of his dancers, Lolly turned to Krejcir for help. Krejcir, in turn, told Lolly's then-attorney, Ian Jordaan, that he had information that could get Lolly out of jail.

Smith deposed an affidavit on 28 February 2010 at the Bedfordview Police Station. The affidavit was apparently so blatantly contrived that Jordaan refused to use it during Lolly's bail application. After his release, Lolly asked Jordaan for a copy of the statement – which he then gave to at least two journalists. Following Lolly's murder, Krejcir claimed that Smith had given him a sworn statement claiming that he (Smith) had been offered money to implicate Krejcir in the killing. According to Krejcir, Czech intelligence agents contacted Smith and tried to persuade him to implicate Krejcir in Jackson's murder with a promised reward of €15 000. Smith would evidently also get immunity from prosecution if he 'signed a statement saying that Radovan killed Lolly Jackson or sent Smith to kill Lolly Jackson', Krejcir claimed. He told several journalists that Czech authorities wanted to use that statement to ensure his extradition.

It emerged that deposing to the so-called 'Kalymnios' affidavit was not the only questionable thing that Smith was prepared to do for Lolly. Krejcir would later claim that Lolly wanted Smith to trash the Teazers Cresta branch run by his former protégé Mark Andrews.

Smith also represented himself as Lolly's 'go-to guy' – the man Lolly would call when he was in a tight spot. He claimed that Lolly once called him after three of his strippers were arrested for stealing underwear from a store at the Eastgate shopping centre. According to Smith, he gave the mall's guards a R2 000 bribe to ensure the girls' release. He also claimed that Lolly had called him out to his home at 4.00 am, following a fight with his wife Demi. Smith said that Lolly had handed him a pillowcase stuffed with cash that he said he wanted hidden so that Demi wouldn't have access to it. Lolly's staff also confirm that Smith organised a Cypriot passport for Lolly which cost him R8 000.

According to Krejcir, Lolly sent Smith to 'punish one guy' and also to 'destroy' the News Café that Kalymnios owned in Kensington.

However, at the time of Lolly's murder, Smith admitted that his relationship with the strip-club owner had degenerated – primarily because of disputes over money. He claimed that the fights centered on Lolly's refusal to pay him for 'rescuing' millions of rands of his money from an international money-laundering scheme.

In the same interview with the *Sunday Times*, Smith portrayed himself as an innocent pawn in the scheme run by Lolly and banker Alekos Panayi. Smith claimed that Krejcir – who had also been involved in the scheme – had suggested that Lolly use him to recover money that Panayi had allegedly stolen from him: 'Lolly came up to me in 2008, saying Alekos sent the money to his father in Greece and because I am a Cypriot, I can get it back. I agreed. He paid me €5 000 to fly to Greece. I managed to get back R37 million. Lolly was happy, but he wanted the balance,' he said, adding that Lolly was 'furious' when Alekos was eventually fired from his bank. '[Lolly] paid his henchmen R10 000 to beat Alekos again. Lolly was aggressive. Alekos agreed to pay Lolly R25 000 a week.'

Smith's claims clearly illustrate that he believed that Lolly was obscenely wealthy. They have also been underlined by forensic probes into Lolly's estate, which revealed that he had R9 million in overseas bank accounts.

Smith claimed that Lolly was obliged to pay him R3.7 million for ensuring the return of his 'stolen' money, but said that he was doing so in dribs and drabs. Smith told the *Sunday Times* that he informed Lolly: 'No, Lolly, this isn't our agreement. There was no trust and, after six months, he didn't pay me. He owed me nearly R4 million – and I didn't have money.'

While Smith has refused to explain his alleged involvement in Lolly's murder, he has hinted that money played a role in the killing. He was quoted in *The Star* in April 2011 as stating that Lolly was 'greedy' and that this may have played a part in his death. His often obscure references to the night that Lolly died have one common refrain: Lolly had 'millions of millions of millions' and Lolly had refused to give him the money he was owed.

In a somewhat garbled interview with *eNews*, Smith began laughing when he was asked about his 'greedy' comment. It became apparent, during that interview, that he had laughed when questions put to him became uncomfortable – and that his laughter had soon switched to anger.

'Please don't push me about what happened that day, please. I'm not that bad person what the newspapers put in in the beginning. Believe me. People who know me. I'm not that aggressive person and I'm not that bad person. Okay, I make my mistakes but I will sort it out, all these mistakes,' he said.

At the time of Lolly's murder, Smith was evidently desperate for money. Once a heavy drinker, he had apparently developed a powerful addiction to crack cocaine. Krejcir would later claim that it was this alleged drug problem that prompted him to sever his working relationship with Smith.

'He was working for me until I found out he had this problem with the drugs so I reject him completely from my life,' Krejcir stated in early 2011. He added that he had been 'apart' from Smith for a year-and-a-half before Lolly's murder because he was addicted to 'the crack'.

'I never invited him for my birthday party, when my son was born, he never been invite,' he continued. 'You know, when I was with Lolly in the Teazers, New Year's party, he never been present because I reject him. Because I try my best before. I was arriving before at the George Smith house to give him sleeping tablets in his mouth, to try to help him. I tell him, "I will take you to the rehab. Detox. I will pay for it." He said, "Yes, I am coming, I am going." He never came there. So when I actually find out he is a wasting of time I just tell him, "Don't come to my house anymore, don't contact me. I don't want to see you anymore" and I reject him from my life.'

Smith clearly didn't get that memo. Just a few weeks before Lolly was murdered, he had asked several criminal advocates to defend him against the 2007 charges that had seen him share a police jail cell with Krejcir. And he also promised that Krejcir would foot the bill.

In addition to his rapidly approaching criminal trial, Smith had other worries. He'd incurred the wrath of Krejcir's associate Cyril Beeka, apparently over a debt he was unable to pay. A week before Lolly's murder, Beeka and an associate confronted Smith at the Harbour Café in Bedfordview. The confrontation became physical and Smith landed up in hospital. At the time of Lolly's murder, Smith's face still bore the marks of that fight.

Months after Lolly's murder, police would investigate reports that it was Beeka who had hidden Smith for over two weeks before the Cypriot successfully skipped the country. Smith later claimed that he was unsurprised that Beeka had died in an apparent assassination because he had become involved with 'the wrong people'.

Smith has never revealed who hid him. He claims that he stayed in a Bedfordview property for 17 days after the murder, before he was able to obtain a Cypriot passport and leave the country through the VIP section of OR Tambo International Airport. Krejcir claims that then-crime intelligence boss Joey Mabasa gave him a detailed account of how Smith had fled: 'He [Mabasa] told me he [Smith] went to the Mozambique. He get a new passport from Mozambique, from Mozambique he went to the uh… Portugal. From Portugal he went to Spain, from Spain he went to Greece, and from Greece he went to Cyprus.'

Police authorities have yet to provide any explanation for how Smith was able to walk through the airport without being identified or apprehended – despite being named as the sole suspect in Lolly's murder.

Smith has offered to tell all about the murder and how he escaped detection – for a price. But not a single South African media organisation has been prepared to meet his asking price of €50 000. There was, however, one person who could persuade Smith to talk, albeit in cryptic innuendo: Krejcir. Smith told *eNews* that he'd only agreed to an eleven-minute interview about reports that Lolly's murder had been an 'accident' because 'Radovan he ask me to talk to you'.

Despite Hawks' spokesman, McIntosh Polela, stating that the unit was looking for the 'people responsible' for Lolly's death, Smith has been reluctant to suggest that anyone else was involved in the killing, which he mistakenly claimed had happened in February 2010:

'Listen, listen. The truth about what happened that day nobody knows. It's only me I know. What

happened last year, it's only me I know. But what the media they say – I was under the drugs influence, I was aggressive person, I was very dangerous person – all this is nonsense, totally nonsense, man. What happened between me and Lolly that day is totally different from what they put on the media, you know what I mean?'

Smith was also adamant that Krejcir had played no part in Lolly's murder. He grew audibly upset when asked if anyone else knew the truth about how Lolly had died, repeatedly stating: 'I don't want to answer that question, I don't want to answer that question.'

He was also wary of confirming that he'd claimed Lolly's murder was an accident. The reported claim appeared bizarre in light of the way in which Lolly had been shot in the back and then pumped full of bullets. Smith, however, has resisted any suggestion that the killing was premeditated:

'Well let me ask you this, let me ask you this. Do you believe, do you believe there was a plan for me to kill Lolly in my own house? [he begins shouting]. Do you believe that he was a plan, he was under a plan to do that, me or somebody else? Do you believe that? Answer to me.'

Smith has also tried to undermine claims that he contacted crime intelligence boss Joey Mabasa to confess to the murder shortly after he killed Lolly. Smith's cellphone records reveal that he contacted Krejcir seven times on that fateful day. After initially claiming that he hadn't spoken to Smith at all on the day of the murder, Krejcir said that he couldn't remember what the calls were about. He maintains Smith called him up to 20 times a day.

At about 6.22 pm on the night of Lolly's death, Smith called Mabasa's cellphone. Media reports claim that Smith sobbed as he told Mabasa, 'I have done something very bad.' The two spoke for 96 seconds and a log of the cellphone tower that routed the call indicates that Smith was not at the crime scene. Mabasa told the *Mail & Guardian* on 4 May 2010, the day after the murder, that Smith had arranged to hand himself over during the call.

But, in a phone interview from Cyprus, Smith attempted to portray this version of events as highly unlikely. 'And from my own place to call Joey Mabasa and after that I must run away. Do you believe that it was under the plan? If somebody he wants to kill someone, he will try to kill him and disappear with no one to know him,' he said.

Smith previously claimed that he and Mabasa had been involved in 'money laundering' together – an allegation that he has never explained and which Mabasa has dismissed as 'rubbish'. Krejcir also referred to claims of corruption and money laundering against Mabasa in early 2011, when he defended the policeman as a 'good cop'.

'But the people said so many stories. Money laundering... I mean the corruption and bullshit. They cannot charge him because it never happened,' Krejcir stated.

Smith has yet to explain exactly what he told Mabasa when he called him on the day Lolly died. When asked why he chose not to stay in South Africa and explain what had happened on the night of Lolly's murder, Smith began laughing: 'This [laughs]... ah man, why I left hey? Cause how can I prove I'm not a... OK, let's put it this way. Like I tell you, Lolly he was very famous person and all this, his activities. Who's going to believe me in that moment? No one.'

Asked if he still believes that, Smith responds: 'Not now. Now I can speak and I have some truth, you know what I mean? That moment I was not thinking very clearly.'

Smith maintains he wants to return to South Africa to explain his part in Lolly's death, but he says he needs money:

> '*I want to say what happened, truth, I want to say what happened. But to say what happened is not gonna be easy, you know what I mean? I want to come to South Africa; I love that country. I love South Africa. But the problem is a financial for me to come back. How to defend myself with no lawyers, you know what I mean?*
>
> '*I want to come back, it's totally true, but I tried to speak to the lawyers. The lawyers they need a lot of money. Which is the right moment? Me and financial are not very good.*'

Smith also faces another major obstacle in returning to South Africa: his own deep reluctance to serve a prison sentence.

The Hawks have acknowledged that Lolly's murder will only be solved if Smith can be persuaded to return to South Africa. Cyprus and South Africa don't have an extradition agreement, meaning that Smith must either return voluntarily or be arrested in a country with which South Africa has an extradition treaty. McIntosh Polela says, 'It is very important that we get George Smith back to South Africa. It is a difficult task but it is a task that we are dedicated to, so eventually we will get him back. He's also desperate to come back to South Africa by the way. It's just that he's scared of going to prison, as he has said in one of our conversations. So we have to find a way to get him back, but we have to emphasise that the time that we used to have people commit murders and think they can get away with it by talking… there's a very limited space for that now and that is one of our difficulties.'

Polela admitted that the '204 indemnity deal' debacle (in reference to the Kebble case) meant that it was highly unlikely that Smith would be offered any deal that did not involve him serving a jail sentence. The former Directorate of Specialised Operations (DOS) offered the deals to Brett Kebble's self-admitted killers in exchange for their testimony against convicted drug dealer Glenn Agliotti. But the evidence given by hitmen Mikey Schultz, Nigel McGurk and Faizel 'Kappie' Smith failed to convince Judge Frans Kgomo that Agliotti had orchestrated what the state claimed was Kebble's so-called 'assisted suicide'. And, to the chagrin of Kebble's family and widespread public outrage, no one was found guilty of the mining magnate's murder.

Asked whether Smith had any chance of securing a 204 indemnity deal, Polela responded: 'Obviously that's the decision of the NPA [National Prosecuting Authority], but the fact that the DOS did it and it went so badly, I think it made us and the NPA think twice about doing so. But I do not speak on behalf of the NPA. They will have to make the decision in the end.'

According to Polela:

'We are always doing something to get Louka [Smith] back to South Africa. I have personally spoken to him on several occasions. The movement in that regard is slow because we have to do everything to the letter.

'As you will appreciate, dealing with a foreign country is always difficult so it will take some time. But we are hoping that there will come a time when George

179

Smith will come back to South Africa because, without him, it is difficult to have the case move forward.

'Even if we didn't [have an extradition treaty with Cyprus], *we will try by all means to make sure that we bring him back because the family of Lolly Jackson wants justice, they want answers as to who killed the father of their family and we owe it to them to bring George Smith back and we owe it to them to prosecute the people who killed Lolly Jackson.'*

Krejcir claims he is doing all he can to convince Smith to return to South Africa:

'I'm trying my best to bring him back, to, to explain to all the people that I have fuck all to do with the Lolly, first of all. Second of all I believe, because I have this experience to run away from the country and to be under the Interpol, is not life. He has to come here and sort out this problem. Either he will seek sometime in the prison...

'I don't know what happened between him and Lolly but he has to. He cannot live like this for the rest of his life, you know what I mean? I have the experience and I will actually be the one who will, uh, advise him. You know what I mean? Not only for my benefit to explain what happened – because it will completely take me out from the picture of the Lolly. But on another side, to take some responsibility because is the right time to say what happened and take the consequences. This is the life.'

In his most recent interview, Smith tried to downplay any suggestion that he would implicate anyone else if offered a deal. He earlier told the *Sunday Times* that he was alive 'because I am not a betrayer. It's not the point about the deal. I don't care about the deal and I don't care about the justice. It will happen, the justice.'

He is also adamant that he has nothing to fear in South Africa and insists he's not in hiding: 'I'm not worried, nothing. I'm not worried at all. Why I must worry? Why? They want to give me a revenge? I'm not worried if I tell the truth.'

Given Smith's apparent history of making sworn statements for cash, he runs the very real risk that his version of what happened on 3 May 2010 – when he finally gives it – won't be believed.

Cyril Beeka

Cyril Beeka was a complex man: a man of few words who inhabited the underworld yet never spent a day in jail, a highly ranked karate instructor, an apartheid struggle hero and an alleged spy with alleged powerful intelligence connections.

But his last moments would be recorded in a tersely worded three-page statement made by the man who watched him die. And that man would later be shown to have lied about his name, his nationality and his past as the convicted assassin of one of Serbia's most feared warlords.

Using the Bosnian name Sasa Kovacić, Serbian Dobrosav Gavrić had fled his native country to avoid a 30-year sentence for the murder of alleged war criminal Željko 'Arkan' Ražnotović and two other men in Serbia in January 2000. He had been living in South Africa, completely undetected by South African authorities, for four years when he drove the car that Beeka was gunned down in.

Initially, police wanted answers about several grams of cocaine found in Gavrić's car and his relationship with Radovan Krejcir – who the Hawks would identify as the prime suspect in Beeka's murder, but who they have yet to question about the killing.

Gavrić claimed under oath that he had known Beeka for 'about a year or so' before the murder and described him as a 'good friend' with whom he'd been in the process of starting a pawn-shop business in Parow, Cape Town. Beeka, by that time, had left his native Cape Town – where his businesses provided security for the city's flashiest entertainment venues and strip clubs – for Johannesburg, where he was not under constant police scrutiny. Authorities were slowly reclaiming control of the Cape Town night life, once governed by the city's underworld. And Beeka was in the line of fire.

It was in Johannesburg that Beeka struck up a friendship with Krejcir. Asked about Krejcir by the police, Gavrić admitted that he knew the Czech, but denied any regular contact with him: 'I have met Radovan Krejcir before and I think it was in Gauteng when I used to play poker. I think I used to have contact with Krejcir telephonically but know I have not been in contact with him in the past nine months.'

The police's interest in Krejcir appeared to be motivated by reports of an alleged altercation between the two men at Beeka's early 50th birthday party at the trendy Casa Blanca in Cape Town. In the midst of dozens of models and half-naked women covered in sushi, things between Krejcir and Beeka turned nasty. Beeka punched Krejcir in the face, splitting his cheek with his ring and thus forcing the Czech to go to hospital. Beeka would later tell sources close to him that he was 'worried' about the fight, which Krejcir has never publicly commented on.

Beeka appears to have been deeply embroiled in the world of Krejcir, Smith and Lolly Jackson – a world that, according to an affidavit by Krejcir's former personal physician Dr Marian Tupy, involved the illicit dealing of gold and diamonds. Beeka's cohorts included Yuri 'the Russian' Ulianiski, gunned down with his four-year-old daughter in a drive-by shooting in Cape Town in 2007, as well as alleged Mafia boss Vito Palazzolo and imprisoned Hard Livings gang leader Rashied Staggie.

Gavrić claimed that Beeka had called him on the day of his murder and asked him to meet with him at the Primi Piatti restaurant at the V&A Waterfront. He agreed and arrived at 11.00 am, when he found Beeka deep in conversation with a man he knew only as 'Sailor'. Gavrić claimed he couldn't understand the conversation because the two men were talking in Afrikaans. When the men decided to leave, Gavrić claimed he told Beeka he would pick up his car from the car wash and then meet him in the road outside the restaurant. Beeka went off to park his car, a silver Audi with no registration plates.

'I... waited for Cyril to come out the parking lot but he was taking long,' recalls Gavrić. After waiting for Beeka to 'meet someone', an exasperated Gavrić eventually called the security boss, who emerged five to ten minutes later and put his bags in Gavrić's silver BMW, 'as he intended to drive with me for the rest of the day'.

After yet more stops and starts, Beeka then directed him to a house where he met with alleged Sexy Boys gang leader Jerome 'Donkey' Booysen – a night-club owner with whom he had reportedly been friends for 12 years. Booysen later took a lie-detector test to show that he had played no part in Beeka's murder.

Gavrić again said he couldn't understand what the two

men talked about because they spoke in Afrikaans, but 'I can, however, state that at no stage did it appear that they had a dispute about anything nor did they raise their voices at each other. It was a pleasant time. I even had a game of pool with Cyril. We left about 45 minutes later and we greeted each other with goodbyes in the normal fashion.'

Beeka then tried to call his brother Daniel who he wanted to visit, but Daniel wasn't home.

'Cyril had turned in his seat with his chest almost facing the driver's side window. I recall this as Cyril was explaining to me about his younger days and the area we were in reminded him of the old days.

'I recall there were two traffic lights close to the house... I recall stopping at one of the sets and I was still talking to Cyril when I saw something stop out of the corner of my eye. The next thing I recall was hearing two loud bangs go off. I was hit in my right arm as well as my left one and I noticed that Cyril had been hit in the chest. It sounded like a shotgun that went off. There was smoke and glass and I was confused by what had just happened. I then came to my senses and noticed a motorbike on my right hand side.

'Then more shots were fired in succession. I managed to first reverse and then put the vehicle back into drive and speed off. The motorbike was then driving in front of me at a very high speed and I was giving chase. I managed to cock my firearm and fired several shots in the direction of the motorbike.

'The next thing I recall was my motor vehicle lifting from the ground and I lost control. Then the vehicle left the road and rolled into the premises of *the University of the Western Cape. I managed to get as far as getting my head and part of my chest out of the vehicle.*

'I was asking for help and I recall seeing Jerome [Booysen] *there as well.'*

Gavrić ended his statement with a line that he would have known to be a lie: *'I have no enemies and I don't know whether Cyril had any.'*

Months later, he would admit under oath that he had been convicted of the murders of Željko 'Arkan' Ražnotović – who he described as a hit-squad commander – and his companions, but would insist that he had simply been 'in the wrong place at the wrong time'. In 2000, Gavrić was a 23-year-old police mobile brigade junior member when he allegedly assassinated Arkan in the lobby of Belgrade's upmarket Intercontinental Hotel. BBC Radio reported that Gavrić walked up behind Arkan's party, and rapidly fired a succession of bullets from his police-issue pistol. Arkan was shot in his left eye and reportedly died in the arms of his wife, the hugely popular folk-singer Svetlana Ceca Ražnotović.

Gavrić has not publicly addressed claims that he was linked to the Eastern European underworld. Instead, he has painted Arkan as a genocidal psychopath whose followers would kill him if he ever returned home. 'Because Arkan was a much-feared hit-squad commander... I fear for my life.'

It remains unclear, if Gavrić's version of events is truthful, why police waited some six months before they arrested him.

Gavrić now claims he fled to Ecuador on the day that he was sentenced to 30 years in jail for the killing because he feared he would be murdered in prison. In 2007, he applied for and obtained a tourist visa to visit South Africa. 'The reason I opted to come to South Africa was because I heard that it was a stable country with new opportunities. I wanted to build a new life and raise my children in a solid society.'

After arriving in South Africa, Gavrić successfully applied for a business visa under his common-law wife's name and began working at a restaurant in Johannesburg. He later began an export/import business. It was during this time, he said, that he was introduced to Beeka.

Gavrić has never revealed whether Beeka knew his true identity. But Beeka had his own secrets: his alleged role as an informant, and powerful links to South Africa's intelligence authorities that were allegedly born out of his role as an anti-apartheid operative. Intelligence boss Mo Shaik admitted that he was friends with Beeka, but denied that he had employed Beeka as a bodyguard at the ANC's Polokwane conference in 2007.

Shaik said that as a 'matter of policy' he could not confirm or deny suggestions that Beeka had worked for the National Intelligence Agency or SASS (South African Secret Service). He told *The Witness* that he was unaware that Beeka had any links to the criminal underworld.

> '*I have heard these rumours, but I didn't get involved in his businesses. My relationship with him was different. I liked his jovial nature... He never asked me to do anything to clear his name; he never asked me for any special favours.*'

Journalist Ray Joseph, who had interviewed Beeka several times, would later categorically state that Beeka had served as an intelligence asset in both apartheid and democratic South

Africa. Beeka, he said, had been allowed to operate various schemes 'in exchange for favours and the information he picked up in the murky underworld of Cape Town'.

Never was this protection more clearly illustrated than when Beeka and four men – all linked to Beeka's Red and Pro Security companies – were involved in a fight in a bar that resulted in the death of a Chinese seaman. The man was so badly beaten that he died of his injuries in hospital a few days after the fight. Beeka went on the run.

Joseph claimed that a senior officer in the police's Organised Crime Unit had angrily told him that authorities had tracked Beeka down but were unable to arrest him 'as he is being hidden away and protected by the intelligence services'. Beeka eventually handed himself over to police but after a number of delays, he was acquitted.

He again made headlines in 1998 when he was allegedly involved in the brutal beating of a woman in a Cape Town brothel. According to Joseph:

'With him on the night was Robert McBride [Magoo's Bar bomber, ANC operative and former Ekurhuleni metro police chief]*, who sat quietly in a corner as Beeka and a Russian man punched and kicked the woman.*

'The woman, 40-year-old mother of two Jennifer Moreira, and Elize Grove-Juries were both placed in the witness-protection programme although Moreira subsequently suffered a breakdown and never testified in court.

'Grove-Juries, who was "cut loose" from the programme within two weeks of testifying, was found murdered in her home soon afterwards although there was never any suggestion at the time that Beeka was

involved. The case collapsed and all charges were withdrawn.'

In recent years, however, Beeka appeared to be keeping a lower profile – and avoiding the courts. He operated as a 'security consultant' and was involved in a number of business deals with Krejcir. These deals included the purchase of property in Cape Town and the attempted takeover of Teazers.

While the Hawks have named Krejcir as a suspect in Beeka's murder, investigators have probed the possibility that he was killed as part of a gang 'turf war'. Beeka reportedly met, at a restaurant in Monte Vista in Cape Town, with a leader of the notorious Americans gang. He was allegedly unhappy over the Americans' apparent attempts to encroach on the Cape Town CBD, over which his security companies had once exercised control.

Joseph writes that he met Beeka in Cape Town a year before his murder – and found a man determined to be recognised as a respectable businessman. He was then the head of security for RAM Hand-to-Hand Couriers which, among other things, services the diamond and jewellery industry and delivers credit cards for major banks.

'He had put on a fair bit of weight, and he appeared relaxed and calm,' Joseph wrote, portraying a man very different from the hot-tempered karate instructor who had once ruled the Cape Town security industry. The man gunned down on 21 March 2011 longed for acceptance in the business world – but seemingly could not escape the violence of the world that had birthed his multimillion-rand security empire.

Beeka's funeral – like his life – would be a mess of contradiction. The service was attended by hundreds of mourners, including President Jacob Zuma's son Duduzane, rugby stars Percy Montgomery and James Dalton, and a collection of Hells Angels. Beeka's wife, ex-wife and children sat in the same row as Natalya, his Russian mistress and the mother of his baby son Timor. Krejcir was unable to attend as he had been arrested on charges of fraud.

Natalya was the only one of Beeka's women to publicly address the funeral-goers. Clutching Timor in her arms, with her head covered by a black scarf, she cried as she described how Beeka had visited his son on the day he died.

> *'On Monday, when he left the house, the last words what he say to his son were "Daddy just love you Timor, I'm yours forever".*
>
> *'My heart is dead on Monday when I'm hearing the news but when I got home and I look into Timor's eyes, I saw that Cyril will live through Timor and Cyril Beeka name will be continued.'*

Beeka's younger brother Edward, with whom he had operated several security businesses, sought to dispel any suggestion that he had been part of the criminal underworld. 'Many of the people who are writing the allegations about my brother are people who never knew him... It really was an honour to have Cyril as a brother.' Edward Beeka said it was fitting that his brother had died on Human Rights Day as he was a 'catalyst for change and fought against inequality... he was a martyr for human rights.'

> *'To those perpetrators that turned their back on my brother, we want to say we forgive you. God is still merciful.*
>
> *'We don't seek revenge but I want to say today that we can cherish and embrace the memories of a great*

man, a man who impacted so many people in a short space of time.'

While the Hawks have claimed that they found a hit list with Beeka's name on it in Krejcir's house just days after he was gunned down, Krejcir hasn't been charged with the murder.

PART III

15

THE KILLING OF IAN JORDAAN AND MARK ANDREWS

The murder of Ian Jordaan came to my attention only a few hours after my co-authors and I had signed the contract to have this book published (21 September 2011). Karyn Maughan had to go back to work, so Peter Piegl and I went to Catz Pyjamas in Melville to have a drink and discuss the way forward. My intention in writing this book wasn't only to share information that I felt would intrigue the public, but also to achieve some kind of personal catharsis. I'd endured months of stress and pent-up emotion and I needed to move on. Expressing all my emotions, thoughts and fears in a book was the best way I could think of to do that.

As we sat on the balcony of the restaurant, wrapping our heads around the monumental project that lay ahead, we felt somehow detached from all the feverish Joburg activity that was going on all around us – it was as though we represented the reason and calm within the chaos. This peace was soon shattered. My phone rang – the voice on the other end of the line belonged to a senior investigator who asked whether I knew about Ian Jordaan's death.

Another call came through – Shaun Russouw from Durban. He too had spoken to the same investigator and also wanted answers. I quickly contacted Mandy Wiener – if anyone would know the facts it would be Mandy, but her phone just rang. A few minutes later, she sent through an SMS saying she was on air and would call back when she could. Unable to wait any longer, I called Paul De Jager who confirmed my worst fears. Ian Jordaan, Lolly's trusted lawyer, was dead.

During the next few hours, I was inundated with questions from the press. I said that while I hadn't been employed by Teazers for seven months, I'd known Ian for some time and mourned his loss. Another call came in – it was Radovan, who said he'd heard of the murder through the radio.

As Lolly's lawyer, Ian had access to R1.8 million that his client had set aside in a trust account pending the outcome of a civil dispute between Lolly and Mark Andrews over ownership of the Teazers Cresta club. According to the Organised Crime Unit and various sources within the media, the funds in this account could have had something to do with Ian's death. Considering how much money had been floating about at various stages within the Teazers' group, this was a paltry sum and certainly did not seem worth the life of a man for whom I had deep respect.

When I heard of the inhumane manner in which Ian had been murdered, I was horrified. His charred body was found on top of the burnt-out undercarriage of his car in Hekpoort on the West Rand – supposedly part of an attempt to make his death look like an accident. His teeth had been removed in a bid to stall identification. I found myself wondering how someone simply needing a quick cash injection could kill another human being so brutally.

Later that evening, forensic investigator Paul O'Sullivan called me at home. He wanted to know if I'd been interviewed on *Talk Radio 702*'s *Eyewitness News*. Unsure of what he was referring to, I said I had limited my statements to comments about Ian as a person and the tragedy that had seen his life end so abruptly.

It had been Mandy who had mentioned the amount of R1.8 million (*see Appendix 9 on page 253*) during our phone conversation when I was at Catz Pyjamas, and I told Paul the cash had been put in trust because of the Mark Andrews' case. The judge had told Lolly to put the money aside to cover any legal fees in case he lost. I seemed to recall that the figure was slightly higher but it was approximately correct. After Lolly died, the money was forgotten, which was why it was still languishing in the trust account.

The previous December, Ian had sent out the end-of-year statements, one of which contained an email referring to this account. I'd brought this to Demi's and Paul De Jager's attention, but it appeared they'd done nothing about it.

The barrage of phone calls continued after my conversation with Paul O'Sullivan. Eventually I went to bed, waking to an article in *The Star* misquoting me as having said I was writing a book about Demi. Talk-show host John Robbie mentioned this on *Talk Radio 702*, so I quickly called in to set matters straight. The conversation began in a cordial manner, but when I said I wasn't aware of Lolly's shady dealings, John challenged me sarcastically. As I've said before, I might have had my suspicions about these, but lacked any evidence until after Lolly's death.

About to settle in to watch the Springboks vs Namibia game, Paul O'Sullivan put paid to my plans when he called, asking me to meet him at his Wynberg offices. Somewhat irritated, I did as he asked. His first question to me was: at what point did I find out about Ian's murder? My answer seemed to displease him; perhaps he expected some revelation that would break the case wide open. O'Sullivan then revealed he'd been hired by Ian's firm the night Ian went missing, and it was O'Sullivan himself who had identified and stopped the transfer of money from the trust account.

The day after Ian's body was discovered, O'Sullivan paid a visit to Demi, who spoke about the book we were writing. Reminding me he was the one to introduce us to our publishers, O'Sullivan strongly suggested that I open up the channels of communication with Demi so we could resolve matters. O'Sullivan told me he wanted this book to succeed as his own tell-all book was to follow ours, and a bit of publicity wouldn't hurt.

I told him that I had no interest in negotiating with Demi as I'd already lost my integrity and was working hard to reclaim it, but added she'd get a right of response. He then told me that according to Demi, I'd signed a non-disclosure agreement while working at Teazers. While this was in fact true, in the end, Lolly had never signed it so it wasn't valid.

Returning to the subject of Ian's murder, O'Sullivan said that, in his opinion, the persons responsible were a group of Nigerians who'd found out about a large sum of money sitting dormant in a trust account. He suspected they'd made contact with Ian and lured him into meeting with them – but he made it clear that no one was above suspicion, including me! At first I was horrified by what I was hearing, but found myself laughing at how ridiculous it was all sounding. I had known Ian personally and had liked the man: how could I

196

possibly have been responsible for such a savage attack?

O'Sullivan countered by saying that he knew Ian had sent me legal letters in an effort to stop me writing this book, implying this was clearly a possible motive for murder. I found his logic faulty – was he trying to say I'd react by killing someone because that person had sent me legal letters on behalf of his client? I confirmed that while I had received a letter, Ian and I were on good terms and we'd even agreed to have a drink together. We were quite capable of separating work from personal relationships. With the 'interrogation' over, O'Sullivan casually showed me a pile of legal folders of Ian's to which he had access. This concerned me somewhat as, some time ago, Sam and I had contemplated divorce and Ian had been representing me. I wasn't entirely comfortable with Paul O'Sullivan potentially having access to such private information.

A few days later, normal life resumed. Peter Piegl and I, along with a friend, Rory, took a trip to Teazers Durban and celebrated what would have been Lolly's 55th birthday. At midnight, I mounted the stage and made the announcement to the crowd, and we all raised a toast on the house to mark the occasion. At breakfast the next morning, Radovan called to say that Mark Andrews – former Teazers Cresta partner – was the prime suspect in Ian's murder.

Mark had been Lolly's best friend, confidant and heir-apparent. It seemed the two had become inseparable when Mark got Lolly hooked on poker. Mark was promoted to general manager, and they later formed a partnership that included the Cresta branch. The fall-out between Lolly and Mark happened for three reasons – Mark was allegedly using drugs, skimming money and dating a dancer: the unholy trinity. Lolly knew this particular dancer as she'd dated Michael Jackson (Lolly's younger brother, now serving time in Malmesbury Prison for the murder of a street child), before he was imprisoned. (*scan QR code 13 on page 219 to access M&G article 'Former Teazers Boss Sentenced to 15 Years'*)

Suspicious of her, Lolly had transferred the dancer back to the Rivonia branch and warned Mark that he needed to change his ways rapidly. But Mark was equally stubborn and played the waiting game. While Lolly was in Greece on holiday around March 2009, Mark brought the dancer back to Cresta. He then changed the name of the venue to Decadence and registered it in his company, Coco Haven. Naturally, this lock-out infuriated Lolly and it kicked off what would become a long and expensive legal battle, ultimately destroying their friendship in the process. Lolly clearly didn't care much about the club, bragging that he'd hold a raffle for it when he got it back – what seemed to aggravate him the most was Mark's betrayal.

Surprisingly, the first round of legal proceedings was won by Mark as the judge found that Lolly had no legal claim to the new business; but Lolly countered with a case against Mark and Coco Haven. Arthur Calamaras, owner of Lonewolf Properties and the Adult World chain of sex shops, was unwittingly dragged into the feud as the Teazers Cresta branch was located in one of his buildings. Lolly felt that as Teazers Cresta didn't pay rent (Lolly had an agreement with Arthur, where Arthur leased offset property in the Atrium Mews, Teazers Rivonia's centre, and Lolly leased offset property in the Cresta centre), Lolly was therefore the lessee, and not Mark. It stood to reason then that in the absence of any lease, Lolly was now losing out on rental fees on the Rivonia Adult World and Private shops.

Ian Jordaan brought this action 'on behalf' of Lonewolf Properties for the eviction of Andrews and club Decadence. The judgment was handed down in early November 2009, and even though it granted Mark the right to sue Lolly for R2.4 million in lieu of renovations (Mark had argued that he'd transformed a 'warehouse' into a club), it also granted an eviction order. Lolly was overjoyed. He immediately told me to scan and email the judgment to the press and waited on tenterhooks until 16 December 2009 when the order became official. Lolly excitedly proclaimed that he'd give Mark's half of the shares in the Cresta branch to Ari Zangas – his Boksburg partner – but Mark seemed to have the last laugh.

As a final act of defiance, Mark gutted the venue; smashing mirrors and ripping out booths. He went so far as to remove the dancers' poles (that had been cemented into the ground) by cutting them out! Even the air-conditioning units weren't spared. When they arrived at the venue on 17 December, Lolly and Ricardo could only stare at the devastation in disbelief. I soon got a call from Ricardo, but could hardly make out what was being said because of the fuss Lolly was kicking up in the background. I was told to bring the video camera and ask Lacksom to join us. On arriving, I witnessed the destruction first-hand. The glass doors that had separated the reception area from the rest of the venue had also been removed, leaving a gaping maw. Mark had even dismantled the light fittings, adding to the gloom.

Ricardo opened a case of malicious damage to property with the Linden police, who took a very disinterested view of what had happened, causing Lolly to explode. Eventually, the police agreed to visit the new business Mark had opened to determine whether he was harbouring any of the stolen items.

To clarify, Mark Israelsohn (part owner of Global Village who had set up a club called The View) had approached

Lolly some time previously with an offer to buy the Teazers' group. Lolly had said that Mark Israelsohn was following due diligence, but it eventually turned out that Israelsohn didn't have the funds.

On Lolly's orders, I was now roped into covert missions to check out The View now that Mark Andrews had joined Mark Israelsohn as a partner – I was to pose as a staff member of Lonewolf. The police questioned Casper de Wet (a former manager of Lolly's who'd remained loyal to Mark), while I was present. Casper said he was aware that property belonging to Decadence was being stored on the premises, but insisted that he didn't know much about it, or if it belonged to Lolly. He added that he couldn't show these items to the police as only Mark was in possession of the keys.

The police said they'd return but never did – a fact that upset Lolly to the end. Lolly then began an intensive search for Mark Andrews but couldn't find him. He became even further enraged when he chose not to go to a poker tournament at Piggs Peak and subsequently found out that Mark had actually been there. A few months later, The View closed down. After Lolly's death, Demi told me that Mark Andrews had come to the house the following Saturday, in a highly emotional state and had offered her flowers, sincerely apologising for all that happened between himself and Lolly.

Some weeks after Lolly's funeral, Ian sat Paul, Demi and myself down and suggested we walk away from the cases that were pending against Mark. This was agreed to and Ian then approached Mark and offered him the opportunity to walk away too – each party having only to cover their respective legal fees. Unexpectedly, Mark chose not to accept – apparently because he needed the money and felt Teazers was now an easy target (*see Appendix 10 on page 254*).

In the early hours of 28 September 2011, a week after Ian's body was discovered, police found Mark Andrews's lifeless body on the desolate R59 highway, between Alberton and Meyerton. Mark's hands were cable-tied and he'd been killed by a single shot to the head. This followed in the wake of allegations that Mark had been involved in Ian Jordaan's murder and, unsettlingly, it seemed that Mark had been on the brink of handing himself over for questioning when he was murdered. (*scan QR code 14 on page 219 to access IOL article 'Curse of Teazers Claims 7th Victim'*)

Rumours that the missing R1.8 million from Lolly's trust account was destined for an offshore account in Mark's name soon began to circulate.

I recently spoke at length with Mark's former partner from King's Paint, who told me that for some months prior to his murder Mark had been in Thailand selling boerewors rolls on the beach, which he supposedly did due to the fact that he was under financial strain and wanted to take some time off. This story was one of many that soon took on a life of its own. Another suggested that Mark had fled to Italy on the night of Ian's murder. On 28 October 2011, Mandy Wiener provided further details on *Talk Radio 702* saying that police had identified a suspect involved in Ian Jordaan's murder. She went on to say that it was a former business affiliate who was involved in a legal dispute over the Teazers Cresta branch. (*scan QR code 15 on page 219 to access EWN article 'Police Identify Suspect in Lolly Lawyer Case'*)

I recall feeling shocked at the time; the implications were severe and had literally painted a target on Mark's back. At the time, whenever the press approached me, I shied away from making any comments as I didn't know Mark very well. I didn't feel it was my place to dredge up the past. The man was dead, and there was nothing to be done about this tragic fact.

On 7 October, I got a surprising SMS from Sharon, Lolly's ex-wife. We'd not spoken for months, after the Jackson family promised her she'd get the much-needed maintenance she was after for her son, Julian – she merely had to distance herself from our book. Sharon's message simply read 'So irritated' and ended with a dismayed emoticon.

I immediately called her and we spent the next hour on the phone. I was sorry to learn that she'd been struggling to get money out of them, despite promises that she'd get what was owed to her son. Apparently, the Jacksons refuted the fact that Julian was a blood relative, claiming he was adopted, and thus wouldn't pay a cent until they received official documentation proving otherwise.

Sharon got into heated SMS debates with Demi, who told her Lolly didn't care for Julian. This was evidently not true as Lolly had on several occasions mentioned that Julian was the only one of his children who loved him for who he was and not for his money. Some time back, when Lolly had agonised over whether or not to send Julian to boarding school, Demi had given Lolly an ultimatum: if Julian were to stay in Johannesburg, she would leave. Demi didn't want children and wasn't prepared to babysit Julian. Robyn and I had tried desperately to secure weekly boarding for Julian in Johannesburg, but all the schools providing this were full and so Bloemfontein was the only option available.

Sharon went on to drop another bombshell – Demi had said that Paul O'Sullivan now worked for her. In hindsight, this might explain why he'd tried to negotiate her interests in the book which it seems she was obsessing about.

The following day I sent Paul O'Sullivan an SMS. He called me and I asked outright if he was in Demi's employ. He flatly denied it, saying she was stupid to be making any such claims as, by doing so, she was putting herself at risk of being included on Krejcir's hit list. O'Sullivan went on to ask how much we'd been offered for our book, and that if I wanted more, I should go and see Demi and try to negotiate a deal. I again explained that money wasn't my motivation and that I was most certainly not going to open myself up to potential extortion later down the line.

On Tuesday 11 October 2011, I was contacted by a warrant officer asking me to talk to him and his colleagues about Lolly, Ian, Mark and other parties of interest to them. Cautious, I had a background check run on the police officers. An investigator confirmed that they were legitimate, and Paul O'Sullivan confirmed that they were members of a task force that had been set up to look into the murders connected to Lolly. Paul called me again that night and insisted it was time to 'come clean'. The task force was after Krejcir and I needed to cooperate or be taken down with him. I told O'Sullivan I knew very little and would neither speculate nor lie. He ended the call and I was left unnerved and worried about my future.

Just prior to our 2.00 pm meeting the same day, an officer touched base to say that the time and venue had been changed: it would now take place at 6.00 pm at their offices. I explained my reservations and opted to meet them on neutral ground at the Eastgate shopping centre. Once I felt more comfortable with them, we shifted the venue to their HQ as requested.

The line of questioning immediately revealed that they meant business:

Q: What is your relationship with Radovan Krejcir?
I explained that he was someone with whom I'd enjoyed a cordial relationship and that, from time to time, we would talk on the phone. The last time I'd seen him face to face was a few months previously when Karyn and I had interviewed him for the book.

Q: You were angry that Ian Jordaan sent you letters about the book?
I denied this, stating that we had a gentlemen's agreement not to let business get in the way of an otherwise excellent relationship.

Q: You were engaged in a sexual relationship with Demi Jackson and that's why you and your wife were going to get a divorce?
I denied this and stated that, to the contrary, our marital hardships had arisen as a result of my getting too involved in my work and consequently having not enough time to devote to my family.

Q: You were angry that Demi promised you the house and then sold it?
Simply put, yes, but it was an understandable human emotion. I felt it was rational to have become upset, given the circumstances, but I'd dealt with it.

Q: There were only a handful of people who knew about the money in Ian Jordaan's trust account?
To be quite frank, many parties were privy to this

information as it had become a matter of public record. Secondly, Lolly liked to brag, which hadn't helped matters much, and thirdly, I was not the only past or present staff member who knew about the money.

Q: You sold information about the trust account to Radovan Krejcir?

I denied this and offered to take a polygraph test at their, or my, expense. I felt this was grossly defamatory and negligent, with no basis upon which to found such an accusation.

Q: You hacked Demi Jackson's email?

I once again explained that while I never had access to her laptop, nor Lolly's post death, I had been instructed by not only Demi, but also by Alan Allschwang to back up Lolly's work desktop computer.

Q: You forged emails pertaining to Demi's personal life?

I stated that I was aware that clearly this question was in reference to an MSN Messenger conversation that had transpired between Demi and her boyfriend four days after Lolly's murder. I countered by asking that, if they thought I was able to do this, would it make sense for me to have been working for Lolly for peanuts?

Q: You were angry that Paul De Jager took charge of Teazers instead of you?

Actually, I felt the next logical 'heir' would have been Ricardo.

They then tried to get me to admit that I knew of the nature of the relationship between Mark Andrews and Radovan, but I stood firmly defiant; I'd never even met Mark. I reinforced the point that I felt a lot of this meeting was centred on the book, and that pressure was being exerted on me by Paul O'Sullivan and Demi, his alleged client. I also raised my concern that, potentially, another will was in existence and that according to Sharon, Demi had admitted as much during a meeting she'd had with Julian. Apparently, Demi told Julian she'd opted not to use this will as, according to it, Lolly's children would inherit nothing. This line of reasoning made no sense to me whatsoever.

The investigators asked me what I thought the outstanding monies owed to SARS amounted to. My surly response was that they should pick a number between R20 million and R400 million. The figure kept changing daily, so they'd have a good chance of guessing correctly at some stage.

Finally they tried to get me to offer an opinion on who killed Lolly. I made it clear that I wouldn't be drawn into speculation. They reasoned that because I was writing a book, I must be investigating the case. This, however, was never my intention. The book was never meant to solve any murders; it was intended to help me get over Lolly's death and shed some light on the events that took place while I was employed at Teazers.

The interview finally ended after three agonising hours.

In hindsight, I felt the 'interrogation' had gone well and went home to inform my concerned wife. The next day, Paul O'Sullivan shattered my peace of mind by telling me I'd actually been a suspect in Ian Jordaan's murder! He said that everyone close to Ian was on the list and needed to be crossed off.

On Saturday night on 15 October 2011, Karyn Maughan said there was a possibility that the *Sunday Times* might run the story detailing me as a suspect and the fact that I'd been grilled at length by the police earlier that week. My natural inquisitiveness piqued, and I decided to call the warrant officer, but he said he was unaware of any such thing and that I should call him on Monday.

Paul O'Sullivan later mentioned that it would have been foolish to run the story, as then anyone who could have appeared on the list – including Demi and Paul De Jager – would have had to be named as well. While he couldn't give me feedback regarding my interview with the police, he informed me that I was no longer a suspect and should just remain calm.

16
IN CLOSING

Undertaking to write a book in just a few months would be an enormous task for anyone, but doing so with Lolly Jackson as the main subject and all the complexities surrounding the world of Teazers, was an entirely different story.

While I'd never take back the lessons and experiences I've gained over the last two-and-a-half years, I do wish that a lot of it never happened.

Death isn't an easy thing to deal with, but it becomes considerably harder when it's vicious, cold-blooded murder, the likes of which I've sadly become accustomed to after that fateful day in May 2010. As a result, I've become almost desensitised to violent crime as those around me have fallen; it never seems to end.

I had thought I was pretty street smart when I met Lolly Jackson; in hindsight I'd no idea about the shadow world that lay just outside the comfort of my own home. I've learnt that murder and money-laundering don't happen in far-away places; they happen right next to us, in pleasant suburbs and to ordinary families.

Johannesburg has a vicious underworld, yet it seems that few ever pay for their deeds. While my eyes have been opened, I'm sure I've not even scratched the surface.

I've often been asked by journalists, friends and strangers whether I fear for my life as a result of having written a book about the underworld in which I've found myself. The truth is yes; at times I've been petrified for myself and my family, but soon realised that there's a time to scratch and a time to back down.

When Lolly died, I looked for answers as I desperately wanted to solve the mystery. I felt I owed it to him to find out what had really happened inside 25 Joan Hunter Avenue that night, on 3 May 2010. It utterly consumed me. But eventually I realised that the truth is whatever anyone wants you to know at any given moment.

Do I believe George Smith killed Lolly? No – the man was an unreliable drug addict and whoever put those six bullets into Lolly was a professional; each one was a kill shot. So who killed Lolly Jackson? We don't know. In the end, if it hadn't been a gun, it would probably have been his own heart.

I've walked away from trying to solve the murder, choosing rather to live in the present. As my late grandfather used to say, 'Rear-view mirrors are for cars, not for life.'

This book has been my own personal rear-view mirror; a way of putting it all behind me so I can move forward.

I don't believe those who carried out the murders – not only of Lolly, but of Ian Jordaan, Mark Andrews and Cyril Beeka – will ever be brought to justice. Besides, it's highly unlikely to have been just one person, and in the end one must ask: does it really matter? What's done is done. Nothing I nor anyone else says or does will bring them back.

Lolly was larger than life and never would have survived if he had lost it all. He'd built an empire to validate his passion for money and power. But while he lived a pretty charmed, fun and over-the-top life, he lost it all in the end.

I like to believe that wherever Lolly is at this very moment, he's at peace but has also realised that in the end, he couldn't take any of it with him – the cars, the women or the money. The more I think about it, the more I don't believe he'd have done it any differently though – he was born to succeed and would pay the price, no matter what. The challenge was far greater for him than the end result. In certain ways, he succeeded in beating the system. Was Lolly Jackson a good or bad person? That's a question I can't answer for you. All I can say is that he was very good to me.

When he died, I was devastated and couldn't see a way forward. But in time, I began to open my eyes to the fact that there were two sides to this man. The dichotomy Lolly embodied is the same aspect of human nature we all have inside us. Lolly simply didn't care who knew either side. If anything, the good was more effectively hidden as the bad shielded him from being hurt.

In the end Lolly Jackson was one of those characters who

unapologetically made a metropolis like Johannesburg come alive, and stimulated others to try to emulate his success. The problem was that he ended up breaking his own rules.

I can now walk away knowing my loyalty to the man who changed my life still stands. My insular, safe perspectives have been replaced with more realistic (yet not bitter) ones. Someday, hopefully not too soon, I'll sit down with Lolly again and ask him what really happened. Until then, I'll remember Lolly Jackson for both the good and the bad, and will endeavour to use the lessons he taught me.

He always used to say, 'When fantasy becomes reality, you lose it all.' Lolly did exactly this and paid the ultimate price.

Love him or hate him, always remember him. The two greatest lessons I took from my mentor were simple rules he never intended to teach me: pay your taxes, and never forsake your family for money.

Controversy is his legacy.

WHERE ARE THEY NOW?

Demi Jackson continues to try to keep the Teazers' group afloat, while attempting to manage the tax liabilities Lolly left behind.

George Smith remains in Cyprus. He maintains that no South African law enforcement officials have met with him in his native country, despite his invitation for them to do so. Smith has, however, had numerous telephonic discussions with officials from the Hawks.

Paul De Jager is now cemented in the role of managing director of the Teazers' group, fighting day-to-day battles that continuously come his way.

Paul O'Sullivan continues to be actively involved in various cases, including Lolly Jackson's, and has a continuing interest in Radovan Krejcir. He has also been active in rhino-poaching investigations.

Radovan Krejcir is currently on trial for allegedly faking cancer to cash in on a multimillion rand insurance policy. His former urologist, Dr Marian Tupy, has turned state witness against him, after concluding a plea and sentence deal with the state. Krejcir has also applied for refugee status in South Africa, but that process has been delayed because a number of media organisations have applied for access to the Refugee Appeal Board hearing.

Ricardo Fabre has recently taken up new employment and continues to try to rebuild his life with his wife and young daughter. Teazers are set to withdraw the case on 13 March 2012.

Robyn Teixeira continues to run her pole-dancing studio, south of Johannesburg. After numerous bosses, she concedes Lolly was her best, saying 'rather the devil you know'.

Sean Newman runs his massage business alongside his family, and now enjoys the luxury of being able to see his daughter grow up.

Sharon Fensham has found peace in the fact that things will never be the way Lolly would have wanted, saying 'Lolly always said he would take it with him. Well, he found a way, didn't he?' She continues to do the best she can for her boys, Tim and Julian.

Shaun Russouw continues to fight Demi and the Teazers' group against what he feels are injustices within the business, with multiple court cases ranging from monies owed to attempted liquidation. He still holds out hope that one day the missing last testament of Emmanuel Jackson will come to light and wrongs will be righted.

ACKNOWLEDGEMENTS

In undertaking a project such as this, it is inevitable that one relies on many people to produce the finished product you now hold in your hands.

The biggest thank you must go to my family. Without the support of my wife and mother, this book would almost certainly not have happened – they've put up with the highs and the lows, selflessly giving of their own time by taking up extra responsibility in our business so that I could follow my dream. We agreed, before I wrote a word, that we would either be in it together or the project would not happen – and neither of you wavered. Without the two of you I would not be the man I am today.

To my co-authors, who picked up on a story not their own and treated it with compassion, often giving me the motivation to tackle the tough bits and get it all down. Peter, you have become a friend with whom I would gladly go into battle; I respect your drive to succeed and willingness to give of yourself, sacrificing the startup of a new business to dedicate yourself to this project on my word – for this I am eternally grateful. Karyn, your care, compassion and slightly stubborn streak has kept me focused on the task at hand; you will forever be the consummate devil's advocate – thank you for caring as much today as you did two years ago.

To members of the media who have so openly embraced this book, often picking up the phone just to check in. Many of you are accomplished authors, and the words of wisdom and advice have been a great source of inspiration. Neil McCartney's willingness to share his photos at no cost is a breath of fresh air; always a gentleman.

To Lolly's friends, family and enemies alike – too many to mention – I cannot begin to express my gratitude for taking my calls and making time to talk about who Lolly was to you – this allowed me to get a full picture of the man. Nichol, Robyn, Ricardo, Radovan and Sharon – thanks for giving so freely of your time to be interviewed, opening up and not holding back, allowing us an unobstructed view into your relationships with Lolly.

A special thank you must be reserved for Shaun Russouw, Lolly's Durban partner of 12 years. Your guidance, stories and assistance have been invaluable. When Peter and I felt lost in the process, you offered us refuge in Durban – the book came together during that time and we cannot thank you and your family enough. I often wondered who was more determined to see this book hit the shelves. We did not always have a great relationship, but you are living proof that truth opens more doors than it closes.

Jacana Media, thank you for being willing to throw caution to the wind and sign us up when others shied away.

To those that I have not mentioned but have played a part, I thank you for sharing this journey with me; it has not always been a smooth one but it has been one hell of a ride.

Lastly, this book would not have been possible without a man named Lolly. Boss, you saw potential in a boy who was desperate, you gave me a chance to grow, teaching lessons no one else did. Without you my life would have been a lot more troublesome, and a lot more boring. Not a day goes by that I don't think about what could have been or about you. We all make mistakes, and if you hadn't ignored mine I would not be the man I am today. May you rest in peace and know that I will forever honour your lessons and continue to be a better man for the chance I was given.

Till we meet again.

Sean Newman

◉

Fables were used in the past as vehicles for passing on wisdom and ethics. I find that non-fiction is a far superior vehicle as it's easier to learn from the mistakes of real people than it is to try making contact with intangible examples. If Lolly's tale has anything to impart, it's that true wealth is found in familial bonds – not in the number of zeros you have on your bank statement.

My thanks therefore go to my wife Precilla, my parents Janos and Marti, as well as to my sister Linda. Their support and belief in me has been unfaltering, and I am the wealthiest man I know for having such remarkable people in my life.

Sean Newman offered me an opportunity of a lifetime when he approached me to become involved in the writing of this book. In the process of creating this work, I gained a friend – a man who has proved himself to be generous to a fault, dedicated, driven and passionate. Thank you for this chance and your belief in me.

Our legal team, consisting of Ian Allis and Jessica James, have been remarkable. Their support and wisdom is unsurpassed and we could not have realised this project without them.

To our publishers, Jacana Media, thank you for seeing potential in us and our story. You took the risk where others faltered and our dream has come to fruition.

My thanks also go to Shaun Russouw for his insight and

support, which has brought much value to our work. Last but not least, thank you to my extended family, friends, Twitter and Facebook supporters and those I might have forgotten to mention – your support has been humbling.

Peter Piegl

◉

To Sean and Peter, we made it through – and we didn't kill each other. I'm grateful for the chance to be part of documenting Lolly Jackson's bizarre life and the people who inhabited it. And I'm glad I got the opportunity to do it with you.

To my family, Mom, Dad, Debbie, Paul and Lee: thank you for always being supportive of my fascination with the dark and interesting aspects of human life. Even if it causes you untold stress.

My work colleagues at *eNews* – Bongi, Cathy, Kerryn, Hajra, Robyn, Mayleen, Zain, Mapi, Nobuhle, Penny, Ben and Patrick – thanks for putting up with sleep-deprived mood swings and enabling me to be part of this project.

Jeremy Maggs – thank you for pushing me to do this.

Nikiwe, Gareth, Andrew, Joanne – thank you for asking the tough questions.

To Kanina (HOP) – you've been a non-stop cheerleader and an amazing friend.

And Shaun… You know why.

Karyn Maughan

QR CODES

Scan these quick response codes with your smartphone to access voice clips, articles and other items of interest as you read through the book.

1

2

3

4

5

6

7

8

9

10

11

12

13

14

15

APPENDICES

Appendix 1 – Map of Lolly's office premises detailing safe arrangements

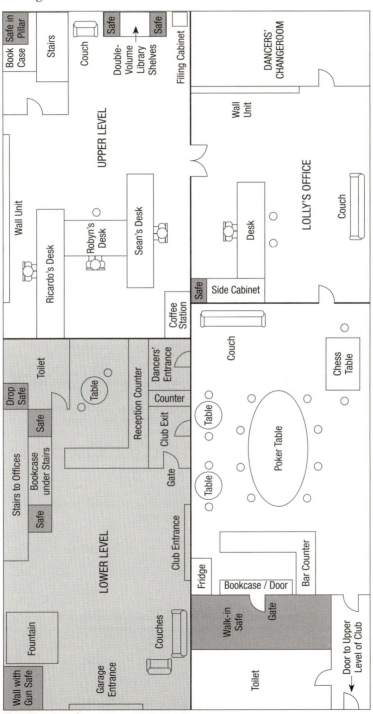

In addition, Lolly had innumerable safes in his two homes.

Note: *not to scale*

Appendix 2 – ASA letters of complaint

Advertising Standards Authority of South Africa

Telephone 011 781 2006 Fax 011 781 1616 Email info@asasa.org.za Website www.asasa.org.za
Willowview Burnside Island Office Park (entrance off Athole) 410 Jan Smuts Avenue Craighall Park PO Box 41555 Craighall 2024
Company Registration Number 1975/00784/08 Non-profit Registration Number 013-694-NPO

PRIVACY AND CONFIDENTIALITY
The information contained in this facsimile is intended for the named recipient/s only. It may contain privileged and confidential information and if you are not an intended recipient, you must not copy, distribute or take any action in reliance upon it.
If you have received this facsimile in error, please notify us immediately on 27 11 781 2006 and destroy the facsimile.

To:	Mr Lolly Jackson Owner Teazers	**Email:**	showgirl@mweb.co.za
Cc:	Mr Ryan Net Director Media Power Solutions	**Email:**	ryan@khulu.co.za
From:	Ms Phumzile Mhlongo		
Date:	23 September 2009		

Reference: TEAZER / ▮▮▮▮▮▮ / 14443

Dear Mr Jackson

We have received the attached complaint from which it appears that you are the correct entity to whom this complaint should be addressed.

Before the ASA formally investigates complaints, we determine whether the complaint is vexatious or *prima facie* without merit in terms of Clause 8.2.1.1 of the Procedural Guide. In other words, we do not formally investigate complaints where we can already tell from the advertising material that the complainant is incorrect or has misunderstood the material. You may be interested to know that in the past year we found that a substantial amount of consumer complaints did not warrant further investigation. To make this determination, however, we obviously need a copy of the relevant advertising.

Please therefore let us have a copy of the advertising referred to as soon as possible by no later than close of business on 28 September 2009. Please feel free to e-mail it to me on phumzile@asasa.org.za and contact detail reflected above.

Should we decide to investigate this matter further, you will be given an opportunity to comment on the complaint at a later stage. While you may make initial comments at this stage should you believe that it is necessary, this is not required.

We thank you in advance for your co-operation.

Yours sincerely
THE ADVERTISING STANDARDS AUTHORITY OF SOUTH AFRICA

PHUMZILE MHLONGO
ADMINISTRATOR: COMPLAINTS ASSESSMENT
CC

Reception

From: reception@asasa.org.za
Sent: 19 September 2009 02:42 PM
To: reception@asasa.org.za
Su ct: Complaint Lodged

Title	
Forenames/Initials	
Surname	
ID/Passport no.	
Address	
Postal code	
Telephone no.	
Fax no.	
Email address	
Company	
Ad Agency	
Type of advertising	Billboard
Where	On Rivonia Road Between 12th and the Spur on the opposite side of the road of Spur.
When	19 September 2009
Who	Teazers
Product	Unknown
Description	The billboard has a woman lying naked on her back with her legs drawn up. The expression on her face is lustfull and she is touching herself between her legs and her other hand is covering only the areola part of her breasts.
Objection	Firstly this advert is sexually very explicit. The expression on her face is very lustfull and she is touching herself between her legs. Secondly this advert is not suitable for children. According to the children's act, children should be protected against There are schools in the area. Thirdly this advert is also objectifying women since it depicts that women are objects of lust and desire.

Lolly Jackson

From:
Sent: 22 September 2009 09:28 AM
To·   Complaint@asasa.org.za
Su~.‚ct: Complaint regarding the Teasers Billboard along Rivonia Road.

To whom this may concern,
I am writing you this letter to complain about the Teasers billboard along Rivonia Road " we don't need gender testing"
I think that this is in disgusting taste on Teasers side, having a mockery on what is going on with Casta Simenia.

Generally the Teasers billboard adverts are bearable, however do not cross the line in terms of naming and shaming. This Billboard has crossed the line and a real person has been insulted. Do not use someone elses misfortunte to there benifit. This is completely disgusting and distasteful. Both on Teasers and Media power on allowing this to be flighted and viewed by many.

Thank you

224

Appendix 3 – Teazers' response to the ASA

To Whom It May Concern.

Please find below our response to the complaint about the Billboard situated on the corner of 12th and Rivonia Roads.

1. The complainant states that the woman in the picture has a lustful look on her face

- If she actually took the time to study the ad she would have established quite quickly that the woman in the ad has her eyes closed and this cannot even begin to be considered lustful. Peaceful is a more appropriate term.

2. The complainant states that the woman in the Billboard is "touching herself between her legs".

- Once again had she taken the time to study the billboard she would have realized that the woman in the Billboard is quite clearly not touching herself unless resting her hand on the side of her leg constitutes such acts as insinuated by the complainant!

3. The complainant states that children should be protected from such things.

- Had this ad been put up by any other company other than Teazers would this complainant had as much to say and complain about. Children are exposed to far worse on the evening news than the sight of a beautiful woman lying on a billboard.

Ads and Editorial for body enhancing products show far more than this particular ad yet they run day in and day out.

The idea that we are harming children by placing this advert up cannot be justified simply by saying so. The complainant obviously has a moral vendetta to the way we operate a clean business and can try as hard as she likes but she will never be able to show one instance that Teazers has harmed a child.

4. The complainant states that the ad objectifies woman.

- Teazers has never in its entire existence objectified any woman. In fact the entire business is built on the idea that woman have power and through that are afforded the opportunity to strengthen their foundation in life in order to move onto bigger and better things.

  Had the complainant taken any time to sit and think about what we stand for she would have quickly realized that Teazers empowers rather than objectifies woman and that sadly for her is the way we have always and will always portray woman.

5. The second complainant states that the Billboard in question makes light of a situation a female athlete currently finds herself in.

- This advert was created before the gender row came to light and its existence and publication is purely coincidental. Teazers is merely trying to assure our valued clientele that we have no inter sexed woman as is so common and disturbingly prevalent in the adult entertainment industry.

  That said at least we tell the truth.

  At Teazers we like to celebrate 100 percent woman and that is a guarantee we give our patrons.

  We are thus trying to show that no false advertising is exhibited when putting up billboards or any other form of advertising.

6. The first complainant states that the woman in the billboard is naked.

- This is far from the truth as had she taken a closer look she is wearing a pair of beautiful shoes that probably cost more than the complainants car.

7. The first complainant states correctly for the first time in her complaint that the woman in the billboard is covering her breasts.

- We wish to thank her for the one astute observation made in her complaint as that is what would have constituted a valid complaint. The pose therefore does not show any form of nudity as expressed in her above comment and therefore does not warrant the time used to type this sentence.

8. All the complaints past and present once again seem to have centered on the female athlete in question.

Please let it be known that since the public and media decided to bring her into this we at Teazers felt it was only fair to give her a gift for her outstanding achievements. This was done not out of guilt but rather because we where seen to be benefitting form her situation, as per point 5 this was not the intention and therefore we have delivered a cheque to her attorneys for the amount of R20 000.

This was accepted by her legal council and the cheque was duly made out to C. Semenya as a token of our gratitude for her outstanding abilities as an athlete and an example to all.

Once again for all the people who have brought her into this, it was never our intention.

Subsequent to reply to all aspects of the complaints I would like you to please take note that the constant harassment my brand receives for every little complaint is totally unjustified and before any further complaints are considered please remember that the constitution of this country quite clearly states that I also have rights.

Freedom of expression.-(1) everyone has the right to freedom of expression,

This includes-

(a)   **Freedom of the press and other media;**

(b) **Freedom to receive or impart information or ideas;**

(e) **Freedom of artistic creativity; and**

(4   Academic freedom and freedom of scientific research.

(2)   The right in subsection (1) does not extend to-

(a)   Propaganda for war;

(6)   Incitement of imminent violence; or

(c)   Advocacy of hatred that is based on race, ethnicity, gender or religion, and that

Constitutes incitement to cause harm.

I as above have the right to freedom of expression through the press or other media unless I contravene the noted exclusions.

I challenge anyone to show me what the Billboard contravenes in order for my freedom of expression to be so grossly questioned?

Please in future consider the above before wasting my time with complaints that have no basis or foundation to even warrant a response.

I once again put forward that since the complainant number one obviously was not offended enough to take note of the advert in question so as to get her facts straight enough to put through a valid complaint.

This in itself means that the complaint is fundamentally flawed and does not warrant any further input from either party.

Complainant number two should stop jumping to conclusions that suit her closed minded side.

Next time Sun International, Clinique or any other company dare show more than a fully clothed woman I will consider sending so many complaints your email server crashes and your receptionist runs for the hills.

I am tired of my brand being attacked for needless and harmless advertising that everyone else seems to have the right to as long as the name Teazers is not attached.

Lolly Jackson

Appendix 4 – Letter confirming Caster Semenya donation

DEWEY & LeBoeuf

Dewey & LeBoeuf (Pty) Ltd.
11th Floor, The Forum Building
2 Maude Street (cnr Fifth Street)
Sandton, Johannesburg
2196

tel 27 11 911 4300
fax 27 11 784 2855

October 9, 2009

Mr. Lolly Jackson
Teazers

By e-mail: sean@teazers.co.za

Re: **Ms Caster Semenya: Payment made by Teazers**

Dear Mr. Jackson,

We acknowledge receipt of your cheque in the sum of R20 000 (twenty thousand rand) drawn in the favour of Ms. Caster Semenya ("Ms Semenya"), as promised by you.

We have informed Ms Semenya of the same and have requested that she provide us with instructions regarding the delivery of it.

We are still in possession of the cheque and are awaiting her instructions herein.

We will revert to you once we receive our client's instructions.

Yours faithfully,

Greg Nott
Managing Partner

NEW YORK | LONDON MULTINATIONAL PARTNERSHIP | WASHINGTON, DC
ALBANY | ALMATY | BEIJING | BOSTON | BRUSSELS | CHICAGO | DOHA | DUBAI
FRANKFURT | HONG KONG | HOUSTON | JOHANNESBURG (PTY) LTD | LOS ANGELES | MADRID | MILAN | MOSCOW
PARIS MULTINATIONAL PARTNERSHIP | RIYADH AFFILIATED OFFICE | ROME | SAN FRANCISCO | SILICON VALLEY | WARSAW

Appendix 5 – Teazers' invitation letter

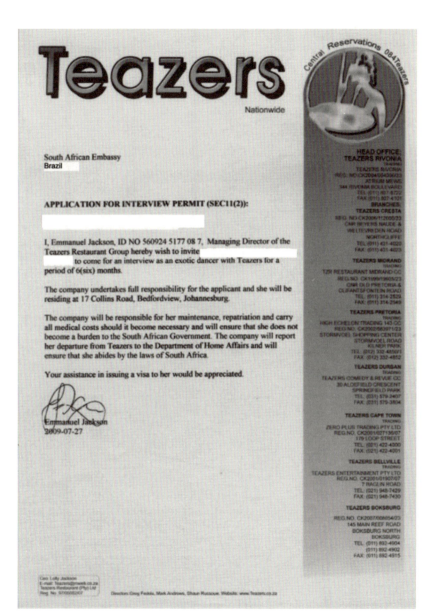

Teazers
Nationwide

South African Embassy
Brazil

APPLICATION FOR INTERVIEW PERMIT (SEC11(2)):

I, Emmanuel Jackson, ID NO 560924 5177 08 7, Managing Director of the Teazers Restaurant Group hereby wish to invite to come for an interview as an exotic dancer with Teazers for a period of 6(six) months.

The company undertakes full responsibility for the applicant and she will be residing at 17 Collins Road, Bedfordview, Johannesburg.

The company will be responsible for her maintenance, repatriation and carry all medical costs should it become necessary and will ensure that she does not become a burden to the South African Government. The company will report her departure from Teazers to the Department of Home Affairs and will ensure that she abides by the laws of South Africa.

Your assistance in issuing a visa to her would be appreciated.

Emmanuel Jackson
2009-07-27

Appendix 6 – Lolly's final cheque

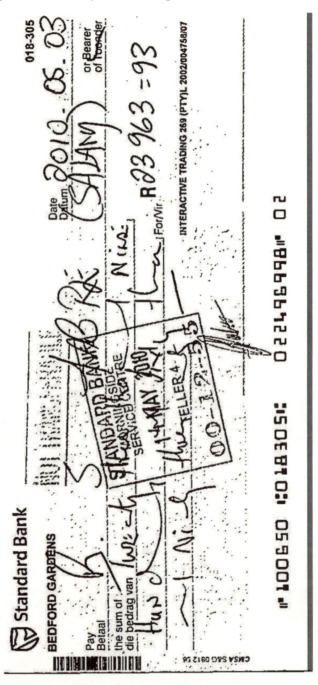

Appendix 7 – Correspondence between Paul O'Sullivan and Radovan Krejcir's lawyers

David H Botha | Du Plessis | Kruger

Our ref:
P J DU PLESSIS/ss

29 March 2011

PRESS RELEASE
29 MARCH 2011

RE: OUR CLIENT – RADOVAN KREJCIR
PRIVATE INVESTIGATOR MR PAUL O'SULLIVAN – THREATS
AGAINST LEGAL REPRESENTATIVES

1. The firm David H Botha, du Plessis & Kruger Incorporated has been instructed by Mr Krejcir to represent him in the matter where he stands arraigned in the Johannesburg Regional Court on charges of fraud concerning an alleged false claim lodged at his insurance company. Mr Krejcir's matter has been postponed to the 7th of April 2011 for purposes of a bail application. Mr Krjecir is held at Boksburg Prison pending his bail application.

2. It has come to our attention that private investigator Mr Paul O'Sullivan who claims to be largely responsible for the investigation against Mr Krejcir and who was also involved in the search and seizure operation at Mr Krejcir's residence, was publicly making threats in the media against the legal representatives of Mr Krejcir. This is seemingly not only aimed against our firm but also against other legal representatives who in the past represented Mr Krejcir. It has to be pointed out that our firm only very recently became involved in Mr Krejcir's defence and that matters pertaining to his refugee status as well as his extradition were dealt with by other law firms. Our firm therefore in the past had very limited relations with Mr Krejcir as a client and any such business was attended to by Mr Ian Small-Smith who has since November 2009 only been a consultant of our firm.

3. Mr Paul O'Sullivan's attack on the legal representatives of Mr Krejcir is, as far as our firm is concerned, without any merit and is regarded as in bad taste. Our firm will not allow Mr O'Sullivan to drag us into a mud slinging match of low morality. Our firm has been in existence as a proud member of the South African Attorneys Profession for fifty years and is known to fearlessly represent our clients as is our duty in terms of the ethics of the Attorneys Profession and as is the right of our clients in terms of the Constitution of the

Established 1960

David H Botha, du Plessis & Kruger Inc · *Reg No. 98/16549/21*
VAT No. 404080012

Directors Pieter Jacobus du Plessis *BA LLB,* Jan Christoffel Kruger *BA LLB*
Roelof Cilliers Krause *Blur LLB,* Edward Stanley Classen *Blur LLB,*
Consultant: Johannes Karel Schaefer Blur LLB Ian Small-Smith *Bproc*

Telephone (011) 838 1214
Fax (011) 836 8740 / 086 603 3183
Email thefirm@bdk.co.za
4th Floor National Bank Building
84 Market Street, Cnr Simmonds
PO Box 8013 Johannesburg 2000
Docex 243 Johannesburg

Republic of South Africa which we respect and uphold. We were never (not even at the height of the apartheid days) and will never be deterred in our duty by any threats of violence or any other underhand tactics by people dissatisfied with the dedication we approach our profession with.

4. Our firm and myself preferred to largely ignore Mr Paul O'Sullivan's antics in the press but it has unfortunately become impossible to do so any further. Today at 11h35 am Mr Paul O'Sullivan directed an email message to writer hereof in the poorest of taste encountered in the long years of my professional life. A copy of the said email is attached hereto, marked annexure A. From the contents of the said email it is unfortunately clear that Mr O'Sullivan has now degraded himself to the level of the worst of violent criminals he allegedly dedicates himself to pursue and is now threatening the personal safety not only of myself but also of my wife and family as well as those of my colleagues. It has to be pointed out that this is the same person which members of the elite unit of the SAPS, the Hawks, chose to take with them on their search and seizure operation at the house of Mr Krejcir. It is to be noted that Mr Krejcir's 18 year old son Dennis Krejcir was (as clearly can be seen from video footage broadcast on e-news) tied up with cable ties and allegedly assaulted and kidnapped as well as threatened with rape to intimidate him to disclose his father's whereabouts. In view of the contents of the email directed to me today by Mr O'Sullivan, it is unthinkable that the SAPS can take someone with that kind of morality with them on search and seizure operations which has to be done with the utmost of care and sense of responsibility.

5. It is to be noted that Mr O'Sullivan has been charged with assault on two people whose property was also searched in his presence by the Hawks the same evening Mr Krejcir's property was searched.

6. Mr O'Sullivan's email directed to me personally with my identity number as well as address and detail of my family, leaves me no alternative but to take him seriously in his threats of violence. It leaves me therefore with no alternative but to approach the South African Police Services and lay charges against Mr O'Sullivan of intimidation. I will not be deterred by the likes of Mr O'Sullivan from carrying out my duties which I undertook under oath the day I was admitted as an attorney of the High Court of South Africa.

Yours faithfully

MR P. J. DU PLESSIS
MANAGING DIRECTOR

"*Annexure A*"

From: Paul OSullivan [flyhigh@mweb.co.za]
Sent: 29 March 2011 11:35 AM
To: thefirm@bdk.co.za
Subject: You have crossed the line

THIS MAIL IS DIRECTED TO PIETER JACOBUS DUPLESSIS ID NO 520929 5035 085

THIS IS A 24 HOUR WARNING NOTICE

IF YOU DO NOT GIVE A SUITABLE RESPONSE WITHIN 24 HOURS, ROLLING ACTION WILL BE TAKEN AGAINST YOU

Hello scum,

Do not see this as a threat - Rather see it as a promise

As a result of the lies you have procured the publishing of, I did call your office, but I see that your operator does not speak English too well, so here it is in a fashion you will easily understand:

When you chose to receive blood money (proceeds of crime - in contravention of Prevention of Organised Crime Act) from Krejcir, that was one thing. That you have chosen to lie for him, is a totally other matter. That you have chosen to lie to the media against me, and persuade your gangster friends to open false dockets against me, makes you move very quickly onto my radar screen, something I am willing to bet, you will wish you had not done.

Its a matter for which I shall now see that you receive the attention you deserve. Attention you will not want, but attention you will get. Unless I receive an undertaking from you by noon tomorrow, that you will never mention my name to the media again, I will take all **lawful** steps to shut you and your crooked business down.

I shall also arange that in-your-face actions take place in front of Cornel, JJ and others close to you. Lying about me, was a big mistake, as all at 36 Sophia street will come to underrstand. When you chose to make it personal, you stepped over a line, a line that will see you regretting your dirty crooked conduct.

I have also been asked (indirectly) by some of the underworld scum out there, the ones that are against your client, to provide personal details of Krejcir and his associates. I'm not sure, but have a nasty feeling they want to do something to him and his asociates. What should I do? Should I include you in the list of Krejcir's associates? after all you have chosen to lie for him, in exchange for his dirty blood money. Please let me know whether I should include your details or not, also whether I should include JJ, or Cornel? Maybe you should just ask JJ and Cornel, whether they want me to give their personal information to Krejcir's enemies. Maybe you should also tell them that you chose to lie about me to the media and to procure false charges against me by your gangster clients, thereby placing them in a position where their lives will be opened up to public scrutiny.

Give the undertaking, or see your business go South, as I will not leave any stone unturned in ruining you and Kruger, Krause and Claasen, should you carry on breaking the law.

2011/03/29

Also, from today, every time you mention my name to the media, I will multiply your conduct by 100 and push it back to you, in a way that will have you reeling. Sooner or later you will realise that I never give in. Never.

Greg Blank, Andre Bouwer, Vito Assante, Jackie Selebi, Mphego and Radovan Krejcir found out th hard way, you have the chance to avoid a big fall.

Read Hosea viii 7

For they have sewn the wind and they shall reap the whirlwind.

Response by Paul O'Sullivan to press release by DBK Attorneys.

Piet Du Plessis, is like his client.

They are both desperate people. I have laid criminal charges against Krejcir's lawyers and have asked them to stop dragging my good name through the mud, despite what they say, it is they that are doing the mud-slinging. Furthermore, they have a strategy aimed at discrediting myself, the hawks and anybody at all involved in outing their client where he belongs, which is behind bars.

Nowhere in my mail have I threatened him with violence. For Du Plessis to say so, exposes himself as a blatant liar.

If he thinks he can make press releases that contain lies, and get away with it, he is mistaken.

Let me deal with a few of the lies in his release:

1. He says they have only recently started acting for Krejcir. This is a lie.

2. He says Krejcir's extradition matter is being handled by others. Also a lie, BDK have been assisting with this for a very long time. In respect of items 1 & 2, I attach just the front page of a letter from BDK, dated 11 August 2010 (almost 8 months ago) Since they clearly did not start acting for Krejcir on 11 August 2010, they have been working for him for a lot longer than *'only very recently became involved'* and it also makes a mockery of the expression *'very limited relations'* when it is clear that the relations are in fact *'unlimited'* and extend to creating false dockets, against myself, as well as making false and defamatory allegations, as well as telling me I am a *'marked man'*.

3. He then says that he will not allow me to drag him into a mud-slinging match. He seems forgotten that it was he who fired the first shot, when he chose to lie about the raids by the Hawks. It seems he is quite accomplished at this and it will be what ultimately drags him down. I ask all journalists and editors to determine if the following is from law-firm that does not want to be dragged into a mud-slinging match, or is from a proud member of the legal profession:

From: ian@myconnection.co.za
Sent: 2011-03-07 11:25:10
To: flyhigh@mweb.co.za
Cc: chrisw@global.co.za;
Subject: Re: Radovan Krejcir

Dear Mr O Sullivan (I use the term very loosely).

I hope in the docket you opened against Krejcir for him threatening you last week you started your affidavit with you being reprimanded by the Hawks for interfering in police investigations, you then anonymously calling me and threatening me, and then my messages to you and so forth.

If you lied in your statement or forwarded a one sided version to the cops you will be dealt with properly.

Consider it a warning and don't for one moment consider that you hold some sort of special lunatic status in law and can get away with your despicable actions.

You have created havoc in the lives of law enforcement officers that once trusted you. You should ashamed of yourself.

Your antics of offering witnesses 204 status haven't gone unnoticed by the authorities either. Keep up the good work. Your threats to others to get false

---

statements out of them will soon be exposed. That is a guarantee.

In the meantime enjoy your free time.

I believe you will soon find yourself on the wrong side of the law.

Let's see how you handle that. Bet you'll then raise an insanity defense.

Ian Small-Smith
BDK Attorneys
Sent from my iPhone

It will be noted that the above e-mail clearly comes from BDK attorneys, the firm that say they do not want to engage in a slanging match.

The same 'professional' attorney said in a later e-mail that I was a 'marked man'.

These are his exact words, which are part of a much longer and insulting e-mail:

From: ian@myconnection.co.za
Sent: 2011-03-07 16:24:56
To: flyhigh@mweb.co.za
Cc: chrisw@global.co.za;
Subject: RE: Re: Radovan Krejcir

Dear Paul,

Its official, there are 5 stooges, not 4. But you are the 'stoogiest' one of the bunch.

You then import a Russian bride?! When is the wedding? What sort of work does she do. (By the way I hear she is a nice girl). You must have bullshitted her on www.iamdesperateandfuckinguglyandneedabride.com .That is the sort of thing lawyers would do, not sanctimonious lunatics like you.

Anyway, I am sure we will chat again soon. In the meantime my buddy, you better hope and pray Selebi isn't acquitted. Either way, from what I understand, you have manoeuvred yourself into the position of a **'marked man'** with your outspokenness, lies and criticism of Selebi and other policemen.

Ian Small-Smith
BDK Attorneys
            Sent from my iPhone

Apart from the obvious proliferation of insulting lies from BDK, they now claim to own the high moral ground and have the cheek to accuse me of mud-slinging.

Du Plessis goes on to say that any attack on his firm is without merit. Yet he remains ominously silent about where the funds came from to keep him and his partners in the lavish lifestyle they have, whilst good South African's are being raped, robbed and murdered, so that Krejcir has cash to splash around on fancy cars, houses and questionable lawyers, the same lawyers are attacking the man that has exposed the dark underbelly of organised crime in South Africa. Is this because their cash-flow is now in danger? I think so.

The same lawyers must know that their client is a man that claims to be unemployed and must also know that the only cash Krejcir has is the proceeds of his evil crime. These lawyers have blood on their hands and they know it. This is why they are attacking the very foundations of the criminal justice system, with their lies and innuendos.

4.   I deny having threatened the personal safety of du Plessis or his family. Once again he is lying for his own agenda. No doubt he is planning some strategy to blame me for the gangster's criminal acts. I am not stranger to false and defamatory allegations, exactly the same happened during Selebi's futile attempts to stop the inevitable.

5.   He says I have been charged with assault against his clients Krecjir's criminal associates. Krecjir's associates have fabricated this and what Du Plessis is trying to do is to give coverage to it.

In summary, it is clear to me that BDK are not the highly professional firm they claim to be. Indeed their conduct is extremely questionable indeed. They are attempting to destabilise the fight against crime and this will be their downfall.

They still have to explain where the funds come from that they use to live such a lavish lifestyle.

I will not be drawn any further on Du Plessis' unlawful conduct, save to say I reserve my rights to take whatever (lawful) action is deemed appropriate as and when it suits me.

Appendix 8 – Breakdown of Lolly's list of bequests

Demi Jackson:

Interest	Bequest	Clause
100%	40 Kloof Road Bedfordview *(Erf 184 Bedfordview)*	6(a)
100%	Right title and interest in Boulevard View Properties CC *(Erf 1629 Bedfordview - No. 9 Skeen Boulevard)*	6(a)
100%	Claims in Boulevard View Properties CC	6(a)
100%	Right title and interest in Teazers Restaurant (Pty) Ltd *(Erf 780 Midrand & Erf 406 Randjesfontein)*	6(a)
1/4	Right title and interest in Teazers Restaurant Midrand CC	6(d)
1/4	Claims in Teazers Restaurant Midrand CC	
	R16 333 (Trust Payment - TZR Restaurant Midrand CC) (per month for 5 years after death) via Samanjul 2 Trust	6(h)
	R16 333 (Trust Payment - Teazers Rivonia) (per month for 5 years after death) via Samanjul 2 Trust	6(i)
	Residue to The Lolly Jackson Trust for Demi Jackson untill her death:	7
	CC's & Companies:	

	Teazers PE CC	
	Teazers Port Elizabeth CC	
	Teazers Rivonia CC	
	Boksburg Teazers CC	
	Teazers Boksburg CC	
	Teazers Cresta (Pty) Ltd	
	Teazers Cape Town Entertainment (Pty) Ltd	
	Actebis 570 CC	
	Netrac Investments No57 (Pty) Ltd *(Helmets)*	
50%	Biker Lifestyle CC *(Advertising)*	
	Red Moonrise Investments 9 CC *(Gate at Rivonia)*	
	Super Car Café CC *(Sports Cars)*	
50%	Café Super Car (Swaziland) Pty Ltd *(Owns Merc SLR)*	
	Teazhers CC *(Name only)*	
	Teazhers Rivonia (Pty) Ltd *(Name only)*	
	Teazers Kawasaki	
	Futuremines Prop *(Property Bellville)*	
	Xanado Property 105CC *(Wesite hosting)*	
	Microzone Trading 964CC	
50%	Rosehip Properties 22 (Pty) Ltd *(Matrimonial home with Demi)*	
	Teazers (Pty) Ltd	
	Teazers CC	
	SDJ Entertainment (Pty) Ltd	
	Tabacconet (Pty) Ltd	

Lakewinds Trade CC	
Bevelblock Brickworks (Pty) Ltd	
AJW Construction Management Consultants (Pty) Ltd	
* We have no Cipro search for the Bold print Companies & CC - We will request	
<u>Motorvehicles:</u>	
Mercedes- Benz Reg no. CTP660GP	
2EM Sporttrailer	
Chevrolet Bakkie - J Viljoen	
Harley Davidson Motorcycle - MF Bender	
-	
<u>Fixed Property</u>	
Erf 2287 Bedfordview	
<u>Issues arising</u>	
Demi has a clear veto in regard to the deceased estate - does she have a veto re the trusts? Yes	
Contents of Kloof. Residue	
Motor vehicles appear to be residue in terms of will and must go into trust - can they be sold? YES	

Foreign estate and SARB regularisation	
Intellectual Property is residue (possibly also cars) YES	
Supercar Cafe is residue YES	
Teazers Rivonia CC is residue. YES	
Bonds and overdrafts? Still waiting on Standard Bank	

Manoli Jackson:

Interest	Bequest to Testamentary trust (untill the age of 30 years)	Clause
1/3	Fixed property known as 200 Westlake *(Erf 200 Westlake ext. 1)*	6(b)
1/3	Right title and interest in Big Name Investments CC *(No. 239 Westlake Hartbeespoort)*	6(b)
1/3	Claims in Big Name Investments CC	
1/3	Right title and interest in Tronic Entertainment CC *(Erf 405 Randjesfontein)*	6(b)
1/3	Claims in Tronic Entertainment CC	
1/3	Right title and interest in Interactive Trading 269 (Pty) Ltd *(Erf 76 Edenburg - no. 344 Rivonia Boulevard & Durban)*	
1/2	Right title and interest in Wollford Properties (Pty) Ltd	6(c)
1/4	Right title and interest in Teazers Restaurant Midrand CC `	6(d)
1/4	Claims in Teazers Restaurant Midrand CC	
	R8333.33 (Trust Payment - Zero Plus Trading) (per month period of 5 years after death) via Samanjul 2 Trust	6(f)
	R12500 (Trust Payment - Teazers Comedy and Revue CC) (per month period of 5 years after death) via Samanjul 2 Trust	6(g)
	R16 333 (Trust Payment - TZR Restaurant Midrand CC) (per month for 5 years after death) via Samanjul 2 Trust	

	R16 333 (Trust Payment - Teazers Rivonia) (per month for 5 years after death) via Samanjul 2 Trust	
	* Incorrectly described Titty Twister CC	
	R25 000 (Trust Payment - TZR Restaurant, Pretoria) (per month for 5 years after death) via Samanjul 2 Trust	

Samantha Jackson:

Interest	Bequest (no Trust) over the age of 25	Clause
1/3	Fixed property known as 200 Westlake *(Erf 200 Westlake ext. 1)*	6(b)
1/3	Right title and interest in Big Name Investments CC *(No. 239 Westlake Hartbeespoort)*	6(b)
1/3	Claims in Big Name Investments CC	
1/3	Right title and interest in Tronic Entertainment CC *(No. 239 Westlake Hartbeespoort)*	6(b)
1/3	Claims in Tronic Entertainment CC	
1/3	Right title and interest in Interactive Trading 269 (Pty) Ltd *(Erf 76 Edenburg - no. 344 Rivonia Boulevard & Durban)*	
1/2	Right title and interest in Wollford Properties (Pty) Ltd	6(c)
1/4	Right title and interest in Teazers Restaurant Midrand CC	6(d)
1/4	Claims in Teazers Restaurant Midrand CC	
	R8333.33 (Trust Payment - Zero Plus Trading) (per month period of 5 years after death) via Samanjul 2 Trust	6(f)
	R12500 (Trust Payment - Teazers Comedy and Revue CC) (per month period of 5 years after death) via Samanjul 2 Trust	6(g)
	R16 333 (Trust Payment - TZR Restaurant Midrand CC) (per month for 5 years after death) via Samanjul 2 Trust	

	R16 333 (Trust Payment - Teazers Rivonia) (per month for 5 years after death) via Samanjul 2 Trust	
	* Incorrectly described Titty Twister CC	

Julian Jackson:

Interest	**Bequest into Testamentary Trust (untill the age of 25 years)**	**Clause**
1/3	Fixed property known as 200 Westlake *(Erf 200 Westlake ext. 1)*	6(b)
1/3	Right title and interest in Big Name Investments CC *(No. 239 Westlake Hartbeespoort)*	6(b)
1/3	Claims in Big Name Investments CC	
1/3	Right title and interest in Tronic Entertainment CC *(No. 239 Westlake Hartbeespoort)*	6(b)
1/3	Claims in Tronic Entertainment CC	
1/3	Right title and interest in Interactive Trading 269 (Pty) Ltd *(Erf 76 Edenburg - no. 344 Rivonia Boulevard & Durban)*	
1/4	Right title and interest in Teazers Restaurant Midrand CC	6(d)
1/4	Claims in Teazers Restaurant Midrand CC	
	R8333.33 (Trust Payment - Zero Plus Trading) (per month period of 5 years after death) via Samanjul 2 Trust	6(f)

Samanjul House OneTrust:

Interest	Bequest	Clause
100%	Right title and interest in Nexor 247 CC *(ATM)*	6(k)
100%	Claims in Nexor 247 CC	
100%	Right title and interest in Scruffy Murphys CC *(Not in name of deceased as on date of death - Liquor licence Rivonia)*	6(k)
100%	Claims in Scruffy Murphys CC	

Samanjul House Two Trust:

Interest	Bequest	Clause
100%	Right title and interest in Teazers IV Durban CC *(Lease for Durban Teazers)*	6(e)
100%	Claims in Teazers IV Durban CC	
100%	Right title and interest in Teazers Security CC *(Employment of doormen)*	6(e)
100%	Claims in Teazers Security CC	
100%	Right title and interest in Zero Plus Trading CC (Teazers Loop Str CT)	6(f)
100%	Claims in Zero Plus Trading CC	
	R25 000 (equal shares to Manoli, Sam, Julian) - iro Zero Plus Trading (per month period of 5 years after death)	
100%	Right title and interest in Teazers Comedy and Revue CC *(Operating Durban)*	6(g)
100%	Claims in Teazers Comedy and Revue CC	
	R25 000 (equal shares to Manoli & Sam) - iro Teazers Comedy and Revue (per month period of 5 years after death)	
100%	Right title and interest in TZR Restaurant CC	6(h)
100%	Claims in TZR Restaurant CC	
	R50 000 (equal shares to Demi, Manoli & Sam) - iro TZR Restaurant (per month period of 5 years after death)	
100%	Right title and interest in Titty Twister CC *(Staff cars & Advertising)*	6(i)
100%	Claims in Teazers Rivonia CC (incorrectly named Titty Twister CC)	

	R50 000 (equal shares to Demi, Manoli & Sam) - iro Titty Twister (per month period of 5 years after death)	
100%	Right title and interest in TZR Restaurant, Pretoria CC *(Profit shareing)*	6(j)
100%	Claims in TZR Restaurant, Pretoria CC	
	R25 000 (Manoli) - iro TZR Restaurant, Pretoria CC (per month period of 5 years after death)	

Samanjul Family Trust:

Interest	Bequest	Clause
100%	Right title and interest in Nexor 247 CC *(ATM)*	6(k)
100%	Claims in Nexor 247 CC	
100%	Right title and interest in Scruffy Murphys CC *(Not in name of deceased as on date of death - Liquor licence Rivonia)*	6(k)
100%	Claims in Scruffy Murphys CC	

Appendix 9 – Proof of R1.8 million in Jordaan and Wolberg Attorneys Trust Account

STATEMENT - TAX INVOICE

LONEWOLF / E JACKSON
INVESTMENT ACCOUNT

JORDAAN & WOLBERG ATTORNEYS &
243A LOUIS BOTHA AVENUE
ORANGE GROVE
JOHANNESBURG
Telephone: (011) 485-1990
Fax: (011) 485-1030

Our Reference: I JORDAAN
Your VAT

Your Reference					Matter	INVESTMENT ACCOUNT				
Our VAT Reg. No. 4500124724		Tax Invoice No.		100134	Date	2010/12/14	Page 1	Account No.	L0000644	
Date	Reference	Details				VAT	Debit	Credit	Balance	
		Balance Brought Forward						1,864,851.93-	1,864,851.93-	

PLEASE NOTE OUR NEW BANKING DETAILS
JORDAAN & WOLBERG BUSINESS ACCOUNT
STANDARD BANK : ORANGE GROVE BRANCH # 004105
ACCOUNT NO: 201 638 266 :FAX DEPOSIT SLIP TO (011)485 1030

		120+ Days	90 Days	60 Days	30 Days	Current	
Total Invested	1,856,852.13-						
Total VAT	0.00	0.00	0.00	0.00	0.00	1,864,851.93-	
Total Incl. VAT	0.00	Items marked with specified VAT % are invoice transactions and include VAT				Total	R 1,864,851.93-

REMITTANCE ADVICE

Please detach and return this portion with payment to :

JORDAAN & WOLBERG ATTORNEYS & CONVEYANCERS
243A LOUIS BOTHA AVENUE
ORANGE GROVE
JOHANNESBURG

P O BOX 46041
ORANGE GROVE
2119

Our Reference: I JORDAAN

Refers to Tax Invoice No.		100134	LONEWOLF / E JACKSON		
	Matter		Date	Account No.	Balance
INVESTMENT ACCOUNT			2010/12/14	L0000644	R 1,864,851.93-

253

Appendix 10 – Lawyers' letter, stating Mark Andrews refused to settle

Jordaan &
Wolberg
Attorneys & Conveyancers

Date:18 October 2010

MRS DEMI JACKSON

BY EMAIL

CC: ALAN ALLSCHWANG

BY EMAIL

CC: SANLAM TRUST LIMITED
ATTENTION: MRS MARIETJIE VAN GRAAN

BY EMAIL: marietjie.vangraan@sanlam.co.za

Dear Madam

LONE WOLF PORPERTIES (PTY) LTD / MARK PHILLIP ANDREWS / COCO HAVEN 1035 CC : CASE NO. 30774/09
COCO HAVEN CC / LONE WOLF PROPERTIES (PTY) LTD (CASE NO: 49206/09) E JACKSON / MARK PHILLIP ANDREWS : CASE NO. 12939/09
E JACKSON / MARK PHILLIP ANDREWS : CASE NO. 9580/09
LONE WOLF PROPERTIES (PTY) LTD / COCO HAVEN 1035 CC & INTERACTIVE TRADING 269 (PTY) LTD : CASE NO. 19454/09

Previous correspondence in this matter refers.

As you know, we proposed to our opponents, in respect of the aforementioned matters, that all of the matters be settled on the basis that each party withdraws their respective claims and bear their own costs.

It was a condition of this proposal that either all of the matters were settled in this way or none at all.

We record that our proposal has been rejected.

In the light thereof, we look forward to receiving your instructions in due course.

Yours faithfully

JORDAAN &

WOLBERG

IN LOLLY'S WORDS

Quotes from the documentary *Life and Times – Lolly Jackson* by Graeme Moon

"*I am here to sell a fantasy. The minute that fantasy becomes a reality I've got no more business. So it's in my interest not to cross the line from fantasy to reality.*"

"*I'm Greek. If I was in a suit, I'd be the accused.*"

"*I get arrested once a year, without fail. It's like my anniversary present; every year I get arrested.*"

"*'My husband came to your venue and now I'm getting divorced.' That's their problem, not mine!*"

"*I take my hat off to my parents – both my mother and my father. They taught me one thing: be responsible for what you do. You make your bed, you lie in it.*"

"*If people sit and think it [the money] grew on trees or I won the lotto, it's not the case. It was perseverance and a lot of hard work.*"

"*It's not only from Teazers but right from the very beginning that I started upsetting people. Wrong, but it's worked for me, because controversy makes things happen.*"

"There was such an opportunity here for somebody who has got the balls and the drive to take this industry and turn it on its head."

"I'm going to be criticised for this one, but what is my stock-in-trade at this business? It's the girls."

"I started my business with nothing; my kids are going to get that from me. I've seen plenty wealthy families give their money to the kids and they've squandered it."

"I sit and I look at Teazers and I say to myself, 'What good am I doing or what bad am I doing? How much good, how much bad?' I think I'm doing a lot better than I am doing bad. Better the devil you know!"

"In this industry, you got to be cruel to be kind. I'm not going to let a girl go out there and she doesn't fit the profile. She's got bad boobs; she's got cellulite that a panel beater couldn't fix. I'm not going to let that girl go out there, it's going to wreck her."

"And the best word that described it all was 'Teazers'; it tells you exactly what it is."

"I sit back and think of the crazy things I did in business to get to where I am..."

"Here's an idea here – let me put up billboards that are going to piss people off and get me more advertising. Fifty-five billboards so far and four have been banned; those four gave me the most mileage."